UNIVERSITY OF VIRGINIA

JEFFERSON'S BUILDINGS AT THE UNIVERSITY OF VIRGINIA

JEFFERSON'S BUILDINGS

AT THE
UNIVERSITY OF VIRGINIA

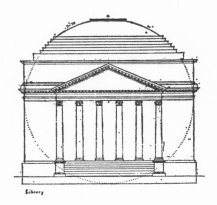

THE ROTUNDA

By William B. O'Neal

THE UNIVERSITY OF VIRGINIA PRESS

1960

For

M. M. O.

FOREWORD

Jefferson, in a report of November 29, 1821, to the Literary Fund, the agency of the Commonwealth from which a large part of the funds for the building of the University of Virginia was drawn, stated that "no considerable system of building within the US. has been done on cheaper terms nor more correctly, faithfully, or solidly executed, according to the nature of the materials used." It is also true that "no considerable system of building within" our country of so early a date has survived with so many and such detailed records of its building. The majority of these records — letters, official minutes of the Board of Visitors of the University, drawings, manuscript specifications, account books and day books — are still the property of the University of Virginia. In this, the first of a series of projected studies devoted to the Jeffersonian buildings at the University, these records are submitted to a detailed examination which it is hoped will reveal the clearest insight into the habits of architectural thought of the University's creator, the difficulties he encountered during its creation, and the many sources from which he derived its specific architectural forms.

In completing a work of this nature, one must rely on the aid of many people. Mr. John Cook Wyllie, now Librarian of the University of Virginia, but during the period of my research the Curator of Rare Books for the University Library, has been unfailingly full of encouragement and wise suggestions. Mr. Francis L. Berkeley, Jr., the University's Curator of Manuscripts, provided the original impetus with his *Calendar of the Jefferson Papers at the University of Virginia* and was never too busy to take time from his many duties to explain obscure points or to aid in the search for documents which might throw further light on specific problems. Miss Ruth Evelyn Byrd, Mr. Wyllie's assistant at that time, sustained the prolonged period of research by her kindness, her knowledge of the documents involved, and her humor. Mr. Frederick D. Nichols, the University's architect for restorations, has been of great help with his continual interest in this project. The staffs of the Library of Congress and of the Avery Architectural Library, Columbia University, should also be thanked for their courtesy, so much in contrast to the lack of that quality at certain very large libraries. The Research Council of the Richmond Area University Center, the Papers of Thomas Jefferson, and the University of Virginia Committee on the Old Dominion Foundation have all very generously provided grants to make this research and the publication of this book possible. I can do no more than express my profound gratitude for their essential and necessary help.

WILLIAM B. O'NEAL
University of Virginia, 1960

ABBREVIATIONS

B of V - The Minutes of the Board of Visitors, University of Virginia. Manuscript deposited in the University of Virginia Library

Doc - Document

JP - *The Jefferson Papers of the University of Virginia. A Calendar Compiled by Constance E. Thurlow and Francis L. Berkeley, Jr.,* University of Virginia Library, Charlottesville, 1950

LC - Jefferson Papers, Library of Congress

pp - previously printed

T.J. - Thomas Jefferson

Note: In printing the original documents, the original spelling and grammar has been retained in so far as is possible with modern typesetting.

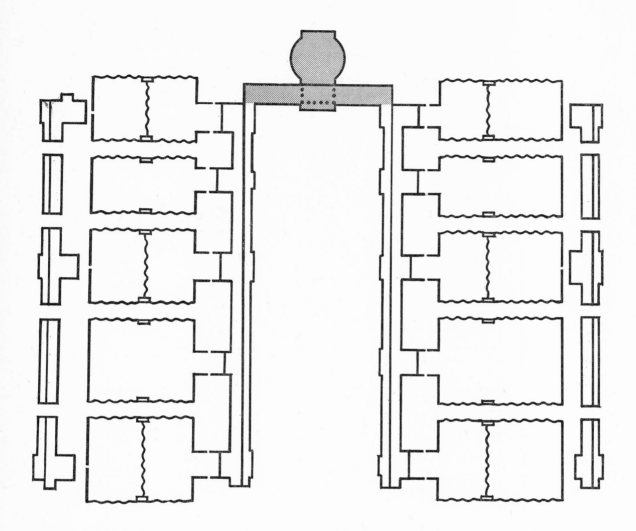

THE ROTUNDA

When the second edition of the Maverick engraving of the ground plan of the University[1] was delivered on March 3, 1825, Jefferson had an explanation of it printed for prospective students[2], an explanation in which he said:

> The ROTUNDA, filling up the Northernmost end of the ground is 77 feet in diameter, and in height, crowned by a Dome 120 deg. of the sphere. The lower floor has large rooms for religious worship, for public examinations, and other associated purposes. The upper floor is a single room for a Library, canopied by the Dome and it's sky-light.
> The Rotunda is connected with the two rows of Pavilions by a Terras on each side of the height of its Basement, and breadth of the flank of it's Portico;

below the Terras is a space for gymnastick exercises, and affording a sheltered passage round three sides of the Lawn, 1400 feet in extent.

A few months later, on November 26, 1825, the Duke of Saxe-Weimar Eisenach saw the University and wrote this less official and somewhat more acid description of the new establishment:

> On the 25th of November [1825] we set out for Charlottesville . . . . About eight o'clock in the evening we reached Charlottesville in which the houses appeared to be scattered. In its vicinity is a new establishment for education, called University of Virginia. The next morning we went to see the University, which is one mile distant from the town.
>
> This establishment has been open since March 1825, and it is said to have already one hundred and thirty students; but a spirit of insubordination has caused many of the pupils to be sent away. The buildings are all new, and yet some of them seem to threaten to fall in, which may be the case with several others also, being chiefly built of wood. The interior of the library was not yet finished, but according to its plan it will be a beautiful one. The dome is made after the model of the Pantheon in Rome, reduced one half. This place is intended for public meetings of the academy: but it is said that an echo is heard in case of loud speaking, which renders the voice of the speaker unintelligible.
>
> Under the Rotunda are three elliptical halls, the destination of which is not yet entirely determined. The set of columns on the outside of this building, I was told is to be a very fine one; the capitals were made in Italy.[3]

The idea for a domical building dominating the Lawn came to Jefferson in a letter of July 24, 1817, from Latrobe, in which a small sketch shows such a building at the central point of the north and closed side of the Lawn. (Doc. 1) Jefferson chose the Pantheon as his model, a building he had studied at least as early as 1791 when he wrote to a book-seller

> . . . . pray get me by some means or other a compleat set of Piranesi's drawings of the Pantheon, & especially the correct design for it's restoration as proposed by I forget whom, which was not executed, & of which I have heard you speak. I wish to render them useful in the *public* buildings now to be begun at Georgetown . . . .[4]

He used the 1721 edition of Giacomo Leoni's PALLADIO as his major source of information for the Rotunda, however, an edition he used throughout the building of the University. (Doc. 26) Even the name "Rotunda" seems to have come from Palladio, for it is used in this description:

> Of all the Temples which are to be seen in *Rome,* none is more famous than the *Pantheon,* at present call'd the *Rotunda* . . . .
>
> The Height of it from the floor to the opening at the top, (whence it receives all its light) is the Diameter of its breadth from one wall to the other: and as People go down to the floor, so antiently they ascended to it by some

2

Steps .... This whole Temple was of the Corinthian Order, as well without as within. The Bases are compounded of *Attick* and *Ionick;* and the Capitels are wrought with Olive Leaves. The Architraves, Frizes, and Cornices, have very fine Moldings, but otherwise little carving. In the thickness of the Wall are certain void spaces left quite round the Temple, both to preserve it the better against Earthquakes, and also to save expence and materials. This temple has a most beautiful portico in front ....

The Stairs mark'd in the Plan on each side the Entry lead over the Chappels in a secret passage, which goes quite round the Temple, and by which one goes out to the Steps, in order to ascend to the top of the Edifice, by other Stairs that are round it. That part of an Edifice, which is seen behind the Temple, and mark'd M, is part of the baths of Agrippa.

This Temple .... has two Frontispieces; the one in the Portico, the other on the Wall of the Temple ....[5]

The Pantheon in the plates in this edition is shown to have a portico seven bays wide and three bays deep, with the rear wall of the Portico flat as well as a flat wall at the rear of the building, this last forming one of the walls of the Baths of Agrippa. The plan also shows curious triangular stairs in the space between the flat wall of the portico and the circular wall of the building proper. It should be noted, too, that it is a perfect circle from the floor to the oculus, a circle whose diameter is the same as the distance between the walls. (Pls. I-V)

Jefferson chose to make his Rotunda seventy-seven feet in diameter, one-half the diameter of the Pantheon, which, of course, resulted in one-quarter the area and one-eighth the volume of the original. (Doc. 93) A Portico five bays (instead of seven) wide, but three bays deep was placed on the south only, with the flat wall retained at the rear. (Pl. VI) The flat wall was retained on the north only after a preliminary, and fragmentary, study in which it does not appear. (Pl. VII) Jefferson added two more floors—a basement and a second floor—and divided the basement and the first floor into three ovoid rooms, while the second floor remained a large circular space with an inner colonnade supporting two balconies for extra book space. (Pls. VI, VIII) The source for the curious ovoid rooms of the basement and first floor fitted within the circle of the Rotunda was probably a plate in Steiglitz. Jefferson had once owned a copy of this book which he sold to the Library of Congress, but he might very well have remembered such an unusual plan form. (Pl. X) The height of the dome is determined by the diameter of the plan, but Jefferson forced the circle to become tangent to the floor of the basement, i.e, to go underground, so that the exterior effect of height is not similar to that of the Pantheon. (Pl. XII) Such a device did allow him, however, to drop one of the two pediments of the original. (Pl. XI) The triangular stairs of the original are forced, because of the reduction in size, into the main body of the building, taking their place quite naturally in the central hall created between the two large ovoid rooms. (Pl. VI)

The specifications on the backs of the drawings work out the dimensions for the various parts both proportionately and in terms of linear measure. Estimates of the brick required appear, and Jefferson was quite definite about using the extra thickness of the flat walls on the north and south, as well as the chimneys, as buttresses. He also explained the method of roof framing, both in a drawing (Pl. IX) and in the specifications. (Doc. 93) He meant, too, to have the interior of the dome painted to represent the constellations and worked out a device which may be described as a saddle on a boom to enable a workman to carry out, somewhat hazardously it would seem, the project. He worried about the relationship of the windows to the volume of the library room, but discovered there was ample glass when the proportions were worked out. (Doc. 94)

The specifications on the drawing for the gymnasia have their dimensions worked out in a very similar way. The floors of the gymnasia were to be level with the Rotunda's basement floor, so that the south wall would be 4' - 2" below the level of the Lawn, its upper portion pierced with semicircular openings. The north wall, due to the change in level, would be completely exposed and consisted of a series of open arches, very like the arcades on the Ranges. They had a flat roof constructed of rooflets and served as the architectural line between the Rotunda and the east and west sides of the Lawn. (Pl. XIII and Doc. 95)

Jefferson's drawing of the bell and clock must have been done at the end of 1825 or the beginning of 1826. (Pl. XIV) His notes include minute directions on the placing of the clock dial, the clock weights, and the bell. (Doc. 96)

The early prints of the rotunda show that each artist had his own ideas as to whether there was or was not a lantern in the center of the dome. Jefferson's drawings prove that he did not want one, although he did install a skylight, as noted in his explanation distributed with the Ground Plan. There was probably never a lantern. At any rate a photograph of about 1870 shows no lantern, although four semicircular ventilators or dormers at the quarter points of the base of the dome do appear. The bell is not in this photograph, but the dial of the clock is enclosed in an archititrave in the center of the tympanum of the pediment and is better proportioned than the existing one. This same photograph also shows a wooden balustrade (*not* a Chinese railing) over the gymnasia.[6]

Another photograph of the same date shows the interior of the library room with its coupled Composite columns and two balcony levels, as on Jefferson's plan and sectional drawing. (Pl. VIII and XII) The balustrade over the entablature of this inner colonnade has turned balusters, pedestals over the columns, and a regular parapet crown instead of a hand rail. The tables then existing (perhaps or perhaps not made after Jefferson's now lost — or possibly never finished — drawing) (Doc.

84) fit arcs of the circle of the plan and seem to have been only at the outer rim of the circle within the colonnade, leaving the center free. The photograph shows the benches, one to a table, were curved to fit the tables and were what would be called American empire today.[7]

The total cost of the Rotunda as shown in the proctor's account books was $57,772.56 as of December 31, 1828.

On March 29, 1819, the Board of Visitors had appointed Jefferson and General John H. Cocke a "committee of superintendance," at the same time appointing Alexander Garrett as Bursar and Arthur S. Brockenbrough as Proctor. (Doc. 2)

On March 29, 1821, the Proctor sent Jefferson a careful estimate for what had so far been called the Library or the Library House. The total of this estimate was $41,299.16. (Doc. 3) At the meeting of the Board of Visitors on April 2, the Board expressed itself as resolved to begin the Library if there were sufficient funds to make it secure and fit for use, but not until the buildings already begun and the western range of hotels and dormitories were provided for from available funds. (Doc. 4) In a letter reporting this action of the Board to General Cocke, Jefferson added that the Library might cost $43,000 and that he was anxious to get the walls up that season. (Doc. 5)

By April 16 Jefferson was asking for estimates for capitals from Appleton. He stated the need for eight pilaster caps and ten full capitals, (Doc. 6) the eight pilaster caps being a number derived from the plan plate of the Pantheon in Palladio. (Pl. I) Not much more was done, however, until the December meeting of the Board of Visitors. Jefferson told Breckenridge on December 9 that the Board delayed the decision for starting the Library until the April meeting, but that all of them thought it should be started. (Doc. 7) The Board did not give the authority to let contracts until its October, 1822, meeting at which time Jefferson asked the Proctor to take provisional bids for the Library. He enclosed an advertisement for the ENQUIRER and the CENTRAL GAZETTE. (Docs. 8 and 9)

In response to Cabell's letter in which he said he was worried by Dinsmore's estimate of the cost of the Rotunda, (Doc. 10) as the Library House was now known, Jefferson answered on December 28 that Dinsmore's estimate of $70,000 was greedy; he quoted other contractors to prove his point; and added that all the costs for it should not run to more than $60,000. This is, of course, the third estimate of which we have a record, each higher than the last. It is in this letter, too, that the Gymnasia are spoken of as covered ways. (Doc. 11)

When contracts for the Rotunda were drawn up as of March 11, 1823, almost six months after the authority for them had been given, the building was called the

5

Rotunda. As much as a year previously Cabell had crossed out "Library" and "Library House" and substituted "Rotunda."[8] It has continued to be called the Rotunda throughout its existence.

James Dinsmore and John Neilson contracted for the carpentry work, with the University buying the materials although they, i.e., Dinsmore and Neilson, contracted for them, supervised and laid off the brick work, and had their prices governed by Philadelphia prices. (Doc. 12) Jefferson approved this contract the next day, adding the cautionary note that the work might be stopped if the funds were to give out. He returned at the same time the contract for the brickwork with Thorn and Chamberlain. (Doc. 13) This same day Jefferson also sent Cabell and all of the Board of Visitors news of these contracts, explaining that they were written in this way because none of the undertakers had sufficient capital to do all the work otherwise, but that they were the only ones who were both available and capable. (Doc. 14) By March 21 James Madison approved the action over the contracts. (Doc. 15) Apparently the other approvals were received, for by April 22 Jefferson was sending the Proctor the exact plates in Palladio to be used as models for the Rotunda entablature, its base, and the entablature for the windows, as well as the architrave for the windows. (Pl. XV-XIX and Doc. 16) Work progressed steadily, since Neilson asked Jefferson about the relation of the floor levels to the sphere of the Rotunda as early as May 5, (Doc. 7) and Jefferson himself sent the Proctor a drawing corecting the angles in the passage by using circles on June 16. (Doc. 18) By July 18, Cabell wrote Jefferson that he, too, was pleased by the progress of the Rotunda. (Doc. 19) In August Jefferson sent the Proctor word that he wanted a folding sash door with a Chinese or iron panel in the Library room over the main door, but forbade a gallery "as that would injure the grandeur of the portico." (Doc. 20) The Proctor had replied by the 11th that the stone sill and window frame for the opening had already been made and that he himself preferred such an arrangement, but that, of course, the door might be used if Jefferson so wished. (Doc. 21) Jefferson answered the same day that he preferred such a door as might be seen in his parlor, (Doc. 22) but a window was eventually used as is shown in the Cook photograph of *ca.* 1870.[9]

In a letter of August 27, 1823, Jefferson told E. S. Davis of Abbeville, S. C., that the Rotunda walls were two-thirds up with the roof to be put on during the next season and the interior to be finished another year. (Doc. 23) By October 6 the walls were ready to receive the roof, according to the report to the Literary Fund of that date. (Doc. 24)

The Board of Visitors, presumably having seen the capitals for the pavilions in place, approved the order for the Corinthian capitals for the Rotunda on October 6, 1823, as well as marble paving for its portico. (Doc. 25) Two days later Jefferson

6

ordered the Rotunda capitals from Appleton, sending careful specifications and references to illustrations as in his earlier order for the Pavilions. He mentioned the omisions as listed in the Proctor's letter of September 20, and explained again the need for the astragal to be a part of the capital block. He asked the price of marble paving for the floor of the portico and enquired about wood Composite capitals for the Library room. (These interior capitals were finally furnished by a Phillip Sturtevant, as shown in the Proctor's account books.) The letter was sent by Giacomo Raggi, who was put under Appleton's superintendance for the execution of the bases of the Rotunda columns, bases which Raggi proposed to make in Italy. And finally he sent a further remittance through Williams of London. (Pl. XX, XXI and Doc. 26) The request for the remittance is dated November 22, 1823, when Jefferson asked the Bursar to put $4,000.00 in the hands of Colonel Bernard Peyton for Appleton. (Doc. 27)

The marble paving was ordered on May 17, 1824, (Doc. 31) and on October 4 the Board of Visitors approved paying for "the articles of marble contracted for in Italy" out of the 1825 annuity if the money could not be found in the subscriptions account. (Doc. 35)

There is a very dry note of one word — "disapproved" — in Jefferson's hand at the bottom of a letter of March 28, 1824, from the Proctor proposing some proportional changes in the Library room leading to the elimination of one balcony and reporting some unauthorized work by Dinsmore and Neilson. (Doc. 28) A letter written the next day by Jefferson rejected these changes and warned that there would be no money to pay Dinsmore and Neilson for work not in their contract. In spite of the severe tone of this letter, Jefferson signed himself "ever & affectionately yours." (Doc. 29)

During the 1824 building season work proceeded rapidly. On April 5 the Proctor sent Jefferson an estimate. Costs so far had been $31,042.72, but the extras of workmen's bills, nails, hardware and painting should not make it exceed $41,000. (Doc. 30) By May 17 Jefferson was able, as already noted, to order the marble paving for the Portico. (Doc. 31) During the first days of June, Thorn and Chamberlain had carried the walls up to the attic, and the Proctor was proposing roof reservoirs for water for fire prevention. (Doc. 32) By the middle of July a question arose about the back steps, (Doc. 33) and by October 5th the Rotunda was roofed, but the interior, of course, was not yet completed. (Doc. 36) The rooms in the basement were for a chemical laboratory and any other necessary purpose; the "open apartments" under the flanking terraces were for gymnastic exercises; the upper circular room for the library; one large room on the middle floor was for examinations, lectures, and religious worship, while the other rooms on the same floor were for "drawing, music, or any other innocent and ornamental accomplishments of life." (Doc. 35)

The first official function held in the Rotunda was a public dinner for La-fayette. Jefferson wrote Francis Walker Gilmer on October 12, 1824, about the plans for the affair, (Doc. 37) and, in response to a toast to himself at the dinner, he stated that he would "cheerfully and zealously" make any possible contribution to the advance of the institution. (Doc. 38)

The 1824 correspondence about the Rotunda ends with a note from the Proc-tor to Jefferson containing the measurements of the dome above the steps. (Doc 41) Before the end of 1824, however, Coffee, the ornamentist, wrote that he would make the rosettes for the exterior of the Rotunda as soon as he knew their height from the portico floor. (Doc. 34) Three months later Jefferson wrote impatiently to know when these ornaments might be in Charlottesville, for the portico scaffolding could not come down until they arrived. (Doc. 39) On December 20, 1824, Coffee re-plied that the rosettes were finished and would be shipped as soon as possible. He in-cluded directions for installing them with round-headed screws to avoid splitting and sent 355 instead of the 330 ordered so that the normal breakage might be cover-ed. (Doc. 40) He wrote again, January 1, 1825, to say the rosettes had been shipped on December 29, and, rather greedily, asked for his money as soon as possible. (Doc. 42) Two weeks later he repeated that the rosettes had been shipped December 29. (Doc. 44) In March he asked for the balance of his payment at once. (Doc. 49) In August of the same year he wrote Jefferson that he had not as yet heard from his estimate for the ornaments for the interior of the Rotunda. Since he had other business at hand, he needed to know about this order as soon as possible so that he could arrange his schedule. (Doc. 58) The Proctor sent Jefferson, on October 1, a triumphant covering note to a letter of Coffee's in which Coffee stated he would do the remaining work for the Rotunda on the University's terms. (Doc. 67)

1825 brought the need for more money. Jefferson told Cabell on January 11 that it would take $25,000 more to finish the Rotunda. (Doc. 43) Eight days later he wrote Cabell again, advising him that the Proctor badly needed $5,000 due on the Rotunda account. (Doc. 45) At the Board of Visitors meeting in March, $6,000 of the money to come to the University from the Federal government was set aside to finish the Library room. (Doc. 46)

In June of 1825 the Proctor asked for instructions as to how to secure the Li-brary room from entry at the head of the steps. He also told Jefferson that Dr. Em-met wanted both large classrooms in the basement, in which case he, the Proctor, thought the museum would have to go to the dining room or the second floor of Pavilion I. (Doc. 51) Jefferson answered the next day agreeing that Dr. Emmet might have both rooms, but suggested that the museum might go to one of the up-per oval rooms of the Rotunda. He thought the wells of the stairs could be secured

8

by balustrades, and he could not come to see about it since he was too ill to ride or drive to the University. (Doc. 52) Two days later the Proctor replied that he meant how should he *lock* the library and asked again how it might be accomplished. (Doc. 53)

On March 8, 1825, Jefferson asked the Bursar to send $3,000.00 at once to Appleton through Peyton and Williams, (Doc. 47) and the next day repeated the request to the Proctor. (Doc. 48) On May 4 a careful statement of the costs of the Rotunda capitals and paving was sent by Appleton, (Doc. 50) and on July 12 a statement of the balance due Appleton was compiled. (Doc. 54) On July 23 Jefferson asked the Proctor the date of the remittance to Appleton. The Proctor was told, too, to get ready to run up the Rotunda columns since all the marble except the capitals was on the ship in Leghorn on April 13. The next day Jefferson also told the Proctor that the bases and pavement were coming on the ship *Caroline* which should have sailed from Leghorn in April, but that the capitals were to have been shipped in May. (Doc. 56) On August 10 Jefferson explained to Appleton that the slowness of the mails had caused a delay in remittances to Leghorn. (Doc. 57) By August 30 he was able to write the Proctor that the bases had arrived in New York and would be trans-shipped at once for Richmond. He asked that special provisions for transport from Richmond be made because of the weight of the cases and suggested that if the shipment must be broken the bases be brought first, so that the columns might be begun at once. (Doc. 60)

By September 6 the capitals had arrived in Boston on the Brig *Tamworth*. General Henry A. S. Dearborn of the Customs House there wrote that they would be sent to Richmond on the first ship, adding that Appleton said they are the "equal in architectural perfection, to any in the U. S." Jefferson made a notation at the bottom of this letter that when the capitals were ordered on October 8, 1823, the tariff was only 15%, but that a new tariff of 30% was enacted on May 22, 1824. (Doc. 61) He sent General Dearborn the invoice on the capitals on September 13, and proposed paying only the duty applicable at the date of the order until Congress might be asked to remit the additional duty, thus possibly saving some $1,200.00. (Doc. 64) On the same day Jefferson informed the Proctor that the capitals were in Boston and asked him to pay Appleton's balance and the duties promptly. In this letter, too, he said the crates containing the capitals were so heavy two ships at Leghorn refused to take them. (Doc. 63) Dearborn, in his answer of the 22nd, suggested that the University should furnish a bond instead of a partial payment of the duties until Congress could be asked for the entire instead of the partial remission of duties, a proposal he made on the grounds that the capitals would present "superb models of antient Architecture" for an educational institution. He included in this letter a careful account of the expenses he had incurred. (Doc. 66)

In the meantime Johnathan Thompson of the New York Customs House wrote on September 9 to say that he had paid the duties on the bases, the pavement, and the mantels for Monticello (included in this shipment for the University), and shipped the crates to Richmond on the sloop *Eliza Allen*. (Doc. 62) On October 3 he wrote again saying once more that he had paid the duties and that he had already received the check for the duties and charges for the Monticello marble. (Doc. 68)

At its meeting of October 5, 1825, the Board of Visitors resolved to ask Congress for the remission of duties on the marble for the Rotunda, to execute the bond for duties pending action by Congress, and to instruct the Proctor to keep a sufficient sum to pay both the old and the new duties if required. (Doc. 69) The Bond, signed by the Rector and the Board of Visitors, was dated October 12, 1825. (Pl. XXII) Three days before this Jefferson asked the Proctor to reimburse Dearborn for the expenses he had advanced on the capitals, (Doc. 71) and on the same day as the execution of the bond he sent the Proctor statements of the sums due Dearborn, Thompson, and Appleton — this last to be sent this time to Thomas Perkins, President of the Union Insurance, Boston, rather than through Williams of London. (Doc. 72) By October 21 Dearborn had the bond and the draft for expenses and was pleased to hear the capitals had reached Richmond. (Doc. 74)

On November 12 Jefferson sent the Proctor a letter from Williams for filing as a voucher. (Doc. 75) Three days later he asked the Proctor what had happened to the money for Thompson, (Doc. 77) but two days after that Thompson wrote that the money had been received. (Doc. 78)

By February 4, 1826, Jefferson had heard that a bill to remit the duties on the capitals had passed the Congressional committee of claims by only one vote and he feared it had a "long gauntlet to run." (Doc. 80) But William Cabell Rives,[10] the local representative in Congress, sent Jefferson word on March 13, 1826, that a bill remitting the whole amount of the duties was passed by the committee of ways and means and was now before a committee of the whole House with a very good chance of passing. (Doc. 81) With this good news before it, the Board of Visitors resolved on April 7 to authorize a clock and bell if the duties were remitted. (Doc. 82) There was a flurry of anxiety about the bond on May 2, for word had just been received from Dearborn that it would be due on the 6th, (Doc. 83) but Rives soon wrote that the bill for the remission of duties on the capitals as well as on the bases and pavement had passed the Senate and gone to the President for his signature. (Doc. 85) Looking forward to the next step in his usual way, Jefferson then wrote to Cocke on the 20th to tell him that measures for the clock might be taken now that the duties on the marble had been remitted. (Doc. 86)

A bell and a clock for the University gave Jefferson a great deal of trouble during the last of 1825 and the last months of his life in 1826. He felt both were essential and wanted the bell to surmount the pediment of the Rotunda, while the clock was to occupy the center of its tympanum. He wrote in August, 1825, to his granddaughter that he expected to hear from her husband about the clock. (Doc. 59) A month later he asked Thomas Voight to send the price of an eight-day clock, as well as the price of both a bell and a proper clock. (Doc. 65) In October he told Coolidge, his grandson-in-law, that the University was unable to buy a bell until more funds were obtained, (Doc. 73) But in November he told his grand-daughter that he expected to be able to order the clock in February. (Doc. 76) On January 3, 1826, he sent instructions to the Proctor to put a temporary bell on the roof of the Pavilion where the books were stored; to protect the rope from "ticklish ringing of students"; and to put a small clock in the window of the same pavilion. (Doc. 79) The Board of Visitors authorized the purchase of a proper clock and bell on April 7, 1826, the purchase to be made after the duties on the marble capitals had been remitted. (Doc. 82) On May 20 Jefferson was able to tell Cocke that the duties had been remitted and that the clock could now be ordered. (Doc. 86) About the same time he told the Proctor that the clock and bell would be ordered, but that he needed the dimensions of the base and the perpendicular of the pediment and the diameter and the depth of the well for the weights. (Doc. 87) By June 4, a month before his death, he was ready to order them from Mr. Willard of Boston, the clock face to be sixty inches in diameter. (Doc. 88) On June 22 he told the Proctor that Mr. Willard would make the clock and set it in place in the Rotunda, as well as order the bell, all of which would probably cost $1,000, a quarter of which must be sent at once through Mr. Coolidge. (Doc. 89) On the same day he sent $250 to Coolidge and promised another $250 later for Willard.[11]

On October 7, 1825, Jefferson reported to the Literary Fund that funds were being used for putting the Rotunda into a "bare state for use." (Doc. 70) By January 3, 1826, he was urging the Proctor to hurry with the book presses (i.e., cases) so that the newly purchased books could be unpacked and put on the shelves. (Doc. 79) A month later they were not finished, nor was the library room yet plastered. A further delay occurred by May, when the roof developed leaks so serious that it probably would have to be re-covered with tin and the plaster then whitewashed. A drawing for library tables was promised at this time in spite of the fact that Jefferson's ride to the University that day had "worsted" him. It was also in this letter that the Proctor was asked to begin the columns. (Doc. 86) Just a little later Jefferson instructed the Proctor to engage Broke to reroof the Rotunda; then to whitewash the dome; and to push the finishing of the Library room. (Doc. 87) He also sent similar information to Cocke. (Doc. 86)

After Jefferson's death the Board of Visitors was able to report on October 7, 1826, to the Literary Fund that the library room was finished. The Rotunda itself was far from finished, however, for the flight of steps to the portico, the marble paving of the portico, the entrance hall, and one small and one large room were yet to be completed. At the same time the question of the location of the museum was settled, for orders were given that the small oval room on the first floor be fitted for the "preservation & exhibition" of the "natural & artificial curiosities." (Doc. 90) Almost a year later the Board decided to have an iron rail installed on either side of the portico to keep people off the roofs of the Gymnasia. (Doc. 91) And finally, a year later, the museum was moved to the small oval room in the basement. (Doc. 92)

The items charged against the Rotunda in the Proctor's account books and Day Book show the multiplicity of interests and abilities of many of the workmen connected with the building of the Rotunda as well as the many sources of materials, since the same names reappear under many of the different items. The greatest number of people were engaged in supplying lumber for the Rotunda. No less than 27 different men are listed: T. Anderson, Nelson Barksdale, W. Black, Ed. Collard, John Crank, J. H. Craven, Thomas Derrette, Thomas Draffin, J. Dudley, Merry Estis, Garland Garth, Willis Garth, Jesse Lewis, Rt. Lindsey, McCall, Rd. McCulloch, Reubin Maury, W. H. Merriwether, O. Norris, David Owens, Pleasants, J. M. Perry, M. Rodes, I. Rogers, Marshall Stone, Lewis Teile, and Micajah Woods.

Jesse Lewis supplied some scaffold poles for $5.60; J. Dudley sold the University some locust posts for $2.00; while the wood for the kiln for drying plank was furnished by Reubin Maury. The plank kiln itself was plastered by Joseph Antrim. And Daniel Arthur hauled the wood to the plank mill.

On December 31, 1826, Dinsmore and Neilson were paid two-thirds of their bill for the carpentry for the Rotunda, as well as two-thirds of half the bill for the book cases for the Library Room. The original sums were $20,821.65 and $585.41 respectively.

The newel posts for the stairs and the interior columns and their bases for the Library Room were turned by Thomas Fadley [Faday ?]. For the newel posts he was paid through Jesse Atkinson, but for the forty columns, with their shafts and bases, he was paid directly ($160.00) on June 18, 1826. A. Hawkins received $26.50 on August 15, 1826, for his 17 days work in assisting with the setting up of the columns and their capitals. The capitals themselves were supplied by Phillip Sturtevant who carved them for $30.00 each. He was paid the full sum of $1,200.00 for these 40 composite capitals on June 17, 1826. The composition ornaments for the cornice were furnished by W. J. Coffee of New York.

Nails were purchased from Brockenbrough and Harvie, James Leitch, Thomas Nelson, and Winn and Davis while the screws came from Alex. St. C. Heiskell and John Van Lew and Co. Both the nails and screws were hauled by Wm. Davis, Wm. Huntington, J. Johnson, J. Moore, and Peter and John Pollock. Brass, copper, and iron wire were supplied by Wm. F. Micose. Locks and hinges were both bought from John Van Lew and Co. Sash weights came from Benj. Blackford; nine dozen window 2¼ in. pullies from Rt. Johnson; glass from Andrew Smith and from Thomas May who supplied two sizes, 16 x 12 and 15 x 12; freight for the glass was paid to I. Acosa, J. Craddock, Crenshaw, J. Makler, and Thomas May. John Van Lew and Co. supplied the glue ($14.30) as well as 12 quires of sandpaper for $4.00. And there is at least one item of $7.87 on December 30, 1825, for smith's work for the shaping of tools and making springs. It is not clear from the account if the smith was paid through Alex. St. C. Heiskell or if Heiskell himself was the smith. Paint and brushes were purchased from C. Z. Abrahams and L. Peck. Linseed oil was supplied by John Garber, Charles Spencer, and John Van Lew. There is also a somewhat mysterious item for "Sole leather for circular brackets" supplied by Saml. Leitch.

Bricks were supplied by both of the principal carpenters, common bricks from J. Dinsmore and both common brick and rubbed stretchers from John Perry. Bricks were also purchased from J. Gorman and Charles Meriwether. Items for column brick, bricks for paving, and rubbed stretchers for steps also appear without their source being mentioned. Thorn and Chamberlain were the principal brick layers. Jefferson was so pleased with the performance of Thorn, that he wrote the following recommendation for him on September 25, 1824:

> The bearer Abia Thorn of Philadelphia, a brick-layer by trade has done much of the brickwork of the University of Virginia, and besides some of the other buildings of the best workmanship himself and partner executed the walls of the principal edifice the Rotunda, than which I believe more beautiful and faithful work has never been done in any country. He is moreover sober, industrious perfectly correct in his habits and conduct of entire probity & worth, and as such I recommend him for any employ he may sollicit.[12]

Thorn and Chamberlain were paid $6,830.72 and $246.76 on November 15, 1823, for having laid 1,025,000 bricks and 50 perch of stone. There is another item of $74.75 for them on February 24, 1824, and on August 21, 1824, their names appear again as having laid the back steps (20,874 bricks), 41 window sills and one plinth for the Gymnasia. Since the item for rubbed stretchers for steps is dated October 24, 1825, more than a year after the above entry, it evidently refers to another set of steps. John Gorman also laid stone for he is credited on May 10, 1824, with having set 21 window sills and the pilaster bases. The window sills were supplied at $5.00 each by T. B. Conway, presumably of Richmond, for there is a charge of $3.00 paid Captain Paine for the freight for 11 window sills from Richmond. The oiling and penciling down of the brick work was done by Benjamin Borden. Thorn and Chamberlain reappear in an item for paving on January 10, 1825, while William B. Phillips is credited on March 21, 1826, with having done the paving in the basement.

The "Labour" account for digging the brick clay for 400,000 bricks amounted to $ 80.00 at 20 cents per thousand. Bricks and rock were hauled by N. Bassett, J. Dinsmore, John Gorman, while Joseph Antrim hauled not only brick but lime and sand as well. Lime was purchased from James Dinsmore, Ira Garrett, Abraham Hawley, M. Jones, John Perry, and Lewis Wayland. It was hauled by Donnie Arthur and John Laurence as well as Joseph Antrim. All or part of the sand seems to have come from the Proctor's land, but Charles Meriwether supplied it. It was hauled to the site of the Rotunda by Robert Ballty, John Pollock, and Mrs. Martha Terrell, the only woman to appear in the Rotunda accounts. Only one name, that of Joseph Antrim, appears in connection with the plastering of the Rotunda.

Iron was supplied by Brockenbrough and Harvie, Jacobs and Raphael,[13] Samuel Leitch, Uriah Leonard, who was a smith, and the Miller Works. Twenty-three bars of iron were purchased from D. W. and C. Warwick on August 19, 1824. Winn and Davis supplied 332 lbs. of iron for hold fasts and girders, while girders were also supplied by Braham and Bibb.[14] There is an item for labor "For making 255 stays for plinths on roof (2 mo. & 14 days work at 19.50 per mo.)" dated December 31, 1824. On June 30, 1825, Uriah Leonard is credited with having made eight keys for the truss girders for the Gymnasia.

The sheet lead for the roof came from Van Lew and Co., but the tin was apparently obtained in New York through Richmond, for there is an item for freight and charges so entered. Sheet copper and tin plates were also purchased from D. W. and C. Warwick on June 17, 1824. Freight for the tin was paid to Harvey Burns, D. Coiner, and J. Cradock, but J. B. Garth is credited with the waggonage for the tin and J. Pollock with hauling both tin and copper.

Anthony Bergamin, "the Frenchman," was the first person to apply the roofing. On September 13, 1824, he was given $ 626.82 for "Copper Roof Gutters, tining on Dome, Cover to Level Cornice, Cutting out Mortar to let in Tin, Gutters to Gymnasia." This resulted in a very poor roof and on August 5, 1826, a confusing item "For the check to Bergamin to make good the roof of dome" is entered. In any case A. H. Brooks [or Broke as he is called by Jefferson] is credited with "Covering the dome." The Gymnasia, too, were either not well done or not completed by Bergamin, since James Clarke is listed for "Pipe & gutters on Gymnasia" as well

14

as for "Pipe & covering of Portico." Lighting rods were also installed as shown by an entry for September 11, 1824, for "Building expences for Franklin rods, crosses, &c. - $ 230.00."

On May 19, 1826, Thomas Draffin, Makains, and John Pollock were paid for the "Rotunda marbles waggonage." And on September 27, 1826, W. W. Minor received $18.00 for hauling "capitels, etc." from Milton, a small hamlet on the Rivanna River, some miles east of Charlottesville.

In addition to these specific items there are unexplained entries for freight paid to Wm. Johnson, of waggonage to C. D. Maupin, and the hire of a carry all from the Miller Works. And finally sixteen cents were paid to John Gorman for the waggonage of a keg of gunpowder.

The Rotunda suffered a great deal of damage in the fire of 1895. The only original fabric to survive is in portions of the exterior walls, portions of some basement rooms, and portions of the shafts of the columns of the south portico. During its reconstruction a portico was added to the north front; the interior was changed from a basement with two floors above to a basement with one floor above; and the interior colonnade was changed from a height of one story with coupled columns to a height of two stories with single columns. At the same time the open arcades of the gymnasia were filled in with offices, balancing wings were added on the north, the connecting arcades between the north and south wings were built, and the whole was crowned by a new marble balustrade.

FOOTNOTES

1. See the Maverick Plan on the endpapers.

2. "Mr. Coffee left Monticello for New York sometime after March 25 [1822] carrying with him Jefferson's groundplan of the University [for an engraving by Maverick] . . . . 200 more copies were delivered March 3, 1825, and these were the corrected ones with dormitory rooms numbered . . . . An 'Explanation of the Ground Plan of the University' was printed to accompany the plan. The two were sold together for fifty cents to students and other interested people . . . . This 'Explanation' was obviously printed to accompany the second edition of the Maverick groundplan since the dormitory numbers used in the 'Explanation' were not on the first edition of 1822-23." pp. 81, 83-85, 86, 87 in Betts, Edwin M., "Groundplans and Prints of the University of Virginia, 1822-1826" in *Proceedings of the American Philosophical Society*, Vol. 90, No. 2, May, 1946.

3. pp. 196-97 in TRAVELS THROUGH NORTH AMERICA DURING THE YEARS 1825 AND 1826, By His Highness Bernard, Duke of Saxe-Weimar Eisenach. Philadelphia, Carey, Lea, & Carey, 1828; 2 vols. bound in 1.

4. p. 371, Vol. IV, Sowerby, E. Millicent, CATALOGUE OF THE LIBRARY OF THOMAS JEFFERSON, Washington, 1955.

5. pp. 74, 75, Book IV, Chapter XX in THE ARCHITECTURE OF PALLADIO; . . . . Giacomo Leoni . . . . MDCCXXI.

6. p. 207 in Kocher, A. Lawrence and Howard Dearstyne, SHADOWS IN SILVER, New York, 1954.

7. p. 208, *Ibid.*

8. JP-1932, pp

9. p. 207, SHADOWS IN SILVER.

10. William Cabell Rives, 1793-1868, U. S. House of Representatives from Virginia, 1823-1829.

11. JP-2328.

12. Jefferson Papers, LC.

13. "Jacobs and Raphael were also Jewish merchants in Charlottesville at that period, and besides their business there conducted stores at Stony Point and Port Republic." pp. 359-60 in Woods, Edgar, ALBEMARLE COUNTY IN VIRGINIA, Bridgewater, Va., 1932.

14. "In 1821 William A. [Bibb] became associated in the mercantile business with his father-in-law, Nimrod Braham. He was appointed a magistrate in the county in 1832 . . . . He married Sarah Braham . . . ." p. 148, Ibid. "Nimrod Braham first appears, when he commenced business as a merchant at the point where the road over Turkey Sag comes into the Barboursville Road. His store there was a noted center for many years. He purchased the place in 1797 from James Sebree and Gravett Edwards. He was highly esteemed both for his commercial skill and energy, and for his civil and military abilities. In 1800

. . . . Lt. in the militia . . . . in 1806 . . . . Col. of the 88th Regiment. In 1801 he was appointed a magistrate. He represented the County in the Legislature in 1812 . . . . He probably removed to Charlottesville in 1806, as he then bought part of the lot on the west side of the Square where for years he did business under the firms, first of Braham and Jones, and afterwards of Braham and Bibb." pp. 148-49, *Ibid.*

18

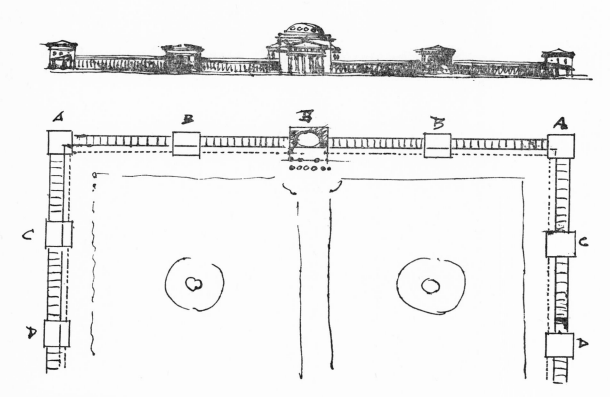

DOCUMENTS

1. Benjamin H. Latrobe, Washington, to T. J.; July 24, 1817; LC

. . . . Center building which ought to exhibit in Mass & details as perfect a specimen of good Architectural taste as can be devised. I should propose *below,* a couple or 4 rooms for Janitors or Tutors, above, a room for Chemical or other lectures, above a circular lecture room under the dome . . . . [See Latrobe's sketch above]

2. B. of V; March 29, 1819

The board proceeded to the appointment of the committee of superintendance, and John H. Cocke and Thos. Jefferson were appointed, with authority jointly or severally to direct the proceedings of the agents of the institution, but jointly only to call a special meeting of the board . . . .

Resolved that Alexander Garrett be appointed Bursar of the University . . . . That the Committee of Superintendance . . . . be authorized to engage Arthur Brockenbrough as Proctor of the University . . . .

3. Arthur S. Brockenbrough, University, to T.J.; March 29, 1821; JP-1854

Estimate of the cost of the Library —
1.050.670 bricks at 11$. p M   11.567.37

10 Bases, 8. half do - 24 Window sills - 2 door do - 1056 feet of steps running measure - Pedestal Coping & base & flaging for portico 2.840.00
Covering dome & Portico with Tin 1.840.00
Carpenters Work & Materials 20 circular Window frames 2 door - 4 front Window do - 2 floor Joists & the entire external finish of Portico, Entablature, dome roof, Attic &c &&c 9.031.19
_____
Total for the Walls & external finish   25.322.86

Carpenters & Joiners work internally. 2 stories
do   do   and materials   7.176.30
for terras on each side   2.500.00
Iron railing   1.500.00
Painting & Glazing   1.800.—
Plastering   2.000.00
Iron mongery about   1.000
_____
$ 41.299.16

The foregoing estimate is agreeable to my best judgement I may have unintentionally omited some of the charges in which I have put down I have endeavored to come as near as I could to the cost. I submit the whole to your better judgement . . . .

4. B. of V; April 2, 1821

. . . . Resolved that it is expedient to proceed with the building of the Library on the plan submitted to the board: provided the funds of the University be adequate to . . . . finish the present buildings . . . . build the Western range of hotels & dormitories . . . . to complete the library to a usuable state . . . .

5. T.J., Monticello, to John H. Cocke; April 9, 1821; JP-1862; pp

Our meeting of the 2ᵈ. consisted of Mʳ Madison, Genˡ. Breckenridge Mʳ Johnson and myself. I send you a copy of our proceedings by which you will perceive important directions confided to us . . . .

With respect to the Library we were all anxious to begin it this year, but equally agreed not to begin it until we have so clear a view of our funds as to be sure they will suffice to finish it so as to be in no danger of asking more money for the buildings. mʳ Brockenbrough has kept only a general account with each Undertaker which does not enable us to know what each distinct building has cost, nor consequently what sum they will cost so as that when they shall be finished we may know exactly what sum will remain for the Library, which we estimate at about 43. M Dollars. he is now engaged in settling the accounts in such form as will give us the necessary information, and let us see exactly the ground on which we stand: so that proceeding no longer on conjectural estimates, we may have the actual expences and payments to guide us. he does not know whether this will take him a fortnight, or a month, or 6. months. but as soon as it is accomplished I will write to you, because our immediate meeting will be necessary. it is wished that the walls of the Library of a million of bricks may be got up this season . . . .

[The following is the enclosure in the above letter:]

Resolved that it is expedient to proceed with the building of the Library on the plan submitted to the board, provided the funds of the University be adequate to the completion of the buildings already begun, and to the building the Western range of hotels & dormitories and also be adequate to the completion of the Library so far as to render the building secure & fit for use: and that it be an instruction to the Comm^ee of superintendance to ascertain as accurately as may be the state of accounts under the contracts already made, the expence of compleating the buildings begun and contemplated; and not to enter into any contracts for the Library until they are fully satisfied that, without interfering with the finishing all the pavilions, hotels, & dormitories, begun and to be begun, they have funds sufficient to put the library in the condition above described.

6. T.J., Monticello, to Thomas Appleton; April 16, 1821; JP-1863; pp

We shall have occasion the next year for 10. Corinthian capitels for columns 32 4/10 I. diminished diam. and 8· D^o. half capitels of the same diameter for pilasters of 30. minutes projection from the wall, to be copied from those of the Rotunda or Pantheon of Rome, as represented in Palladio. Be so good as to inform me what will be their exact cost, ...

7. T.J., Monticello, to James Breckenridge; Dec. 9, 1821; JP-1909; pp

. . . . we suspended a decision on commencing the Library until April when we hope to have a full meeting . . . . we are all decidely of opinion we ought to begin it if we can be sure of being able to raise the walls and roof them so as to keep them safe.

8. B of V, T.J.'s hand; Oct. 7, 1822

Resolved that the Proctor be instructed to enter into conferences with such skillful and responsible undertakers as he would approve, for the building of the Library, on the plan heretofore proposed and now in his possission, and to procure from them declarations of the smallest sums for which they will undertake the different portions of the work of the said building, each portion to be done as well, in materials, manner, and sufficiency, as the best of the same kind of work already done in the preceeding buildings, or as well & sufficiently as shall now be agreed on . . . .

9. T.J., Monticello, to Arthur S. Brockenbrough; Oct. 11, 1822; JP-1949

I transcribe for your information a resolution of the Visitors of the University entered into at their late meeting, to which they recommend your early attention· Also a copy of an advertisement to be published in the Enquirer and Central gazette.
At a meeting of the Visitors &c. on Monday the 7th. of October. 1822
Resolved that the Proctor be instructed to enter into conferences with such

skilful and responsible undertakers as he would approve for the building of the Library, on the plan heretofore proposed, and now in his possision, and to procure from them declarations of the smallest sums for which they will undertake the different portions of the work of the said building, each portion to be done as well, in materials, manner & sufficiency, as the best of the same kind of work already done in the preceeding buildings, or as well and sufficiently as shall now be agreed on: that (omitting the capitels of the columns, which would be procured elsewhere) the several other portions be specified under such general heads and details as may be convenient to shew the cost of each, and by whom undertaken, fixing also the time within which each portion shall be compleated: and that his agreements be provisional only, and subject to the future acceptance or refusal of the Visitors.

[The following is a fragment of a copy in the Proctor's hand of the enclosed advertisement:]

Not a single samel brick to be used not more than 2 bats in ten bricks the bond to be header & stretcher through the whole thickness and on every course of bricks to be solidly grouted the cement 2/3 sand & 1/3 lime sand the wall to be ½ a brick thicker than in the drawings to be added inside — the outer bricks uniform in color and of the color of Pavilions 2 and 4 —, the brickwork to be contracted for to the top of the Corinthian cornice only at first — the carpenters to have a right to examin the correctness of the work as it goes on and to *notify* the Proctor in time for correction if anything be going on wrong The plank used for the Carpenters to be completely seasoned — the ribs of the roof to be completely semi-circular of 4 thicknesses breaking joints — the curbed plate of 4 thicknesses also of 3 Inch thick breaking joints and iron bolted the first undertaking to be only of the walls, roof Corinthian entablature, windows, doors, floors & staircases The carpenters work at the printed prices and Where not specified among them to be settled before hand.

10. Joseph C. Cabell, Richmond, to T.J.; Dec. 23, 1822; JP-1958; pp

Mr. Gordon & Mr. Rives left this for Albemarle on yesterday and will not probably return for eight or ten days. The latter went for his family, & the former to visit Mrs. Gordon in her distress for the loss of a child. I am very sorry that they were obliged to leave town, as we want the aid of all our friends at this time.

Mr. Gordon shewed me on Saturday a letter which he had just received from Mr. Dinsmore stating that the undertakers had ascertained that they could not afford to build the Library for less than $ 70,000. At my instance, Mr. Gordon threw the letter in the fire. My object was to prevent it being made an improper use of, in the event of its being seen by our enemies. I have spoken with one or two friends confidentially on this subject, and we all agree if the price of the undertakers should rise above $ 50,000, & more especially if it should reach $70,000, it would be better to abadon the project of a conditional contract on their parts, and leave us at large. In our opinion we should not ask for more than $ 50,000. for the library, suggesting that if the Job should be put up to the lowest bidder among the workmen of the first rate ability in the U. States that sum would probably suffice, & if it should fall short, the deficiency could be made up from the annuity or from some other source· At all events we would hope not to trouble the Legislature again on that subject. *If matters have not gone too far,* we would prefer that no such document as one calling for $ 70,000, for the Library should be sent here. It would probably blow up all our plans. Perhaps a conditional contract for $ 60,000 might not do harm, as it would bar the door to all doubt about the price of the House. but if $70,000. should be asked for, I fear we shall be totally overthrown. Could you not reject the offer of the undertakers *on the ground that we may be able to get better terms* & authorize me by letter to ask for $ 50,000. for the Library? I suggest these ideas with deference to your better judgement.- I should observe to you that even now there is a great hesitancy in the ranks of our friends as to the propriety of building the Library at this time: this too, while the belief is that it would cost at most about $ 50,000. One or two of my best friends in the Assembly tell me they think that many who would vote for cancelling the debt would oppose any further appropriation for building. I am endeavoring to remove the objections, but am uncertain how far I shall be able to succeed.

What I think of at present is to ask for the 1st proposition in my last letter: that is to cancel & appropriate both. The ways & means which I now contemplate are to ask for a Loan of $ 50,000. out of the *surplus capital on hand,* to build the Library; and then put the whole debt of the University, thus augmented to $ 170,000. along with the other debts of the state, under the operation of the sinking fund. I have latterly struck on this plan on consultation with your grandson, who suggested the idea of resorting to the sinking fund. I have mentioned it to Mr. Loyall, Mr. Boyer, & Mr. Hunter who all, on first view, highly approve it. On the best reflection I can give the subject, it is the best plan we can adopt. We had better let the Literary fund stand as it is - not intermeddle with the provision for the schools, or the surplus appropriated to the Colleges. Let us know nothing to do with old balances, or dead horses, or escheated lands, but ask boldly to be exonerated from our debts by the powerful sinking fund of the state. This is manly & dignified legislation, & if we fail, the blame will not be ours. Such are my present views. Some there are who think we had better ask for the Loan only, at this time, and leave the debt for another session. There are arguments for & agt. this course. It would lessen the present demand. But it would leave the door open for future applications & postpone the time of our commencement. The public mind seems impatient for a commencement of the operations of the institution. My present impressions are in favor of asking for the whole. - I think it would be important to shew that if we could finish the buildings & get rid of the debt we could go without troubling the Assembly again. There are some who say, 'you will want a Library & apparatus, and you will be obliged to come here for more money, & is it not better to expend the $ 50,000 in that way, than in buildings?' I am taking *this* ground - that no doubt occasional gifts from the Legislature for the purchase of books & apparatus would be of service and of great importance: but that we could get along without them, by appropriating half the fees of tuition to that object, & that we have already adopted a resolution whereby half the fees will go into the coffers of the Institution: And that we had rather have $ 50,000. to finish the buildings, than to purchase books & apparatus. I should wish to be corrected if I err on any of these important points.

I have very great confidence in Mr. Hunter. Last night he pressed me to write for the Report. He says members will take time to consider the subject, and there is no time to lose. Unfortunately the question ab^t. the seat of Gov^t. is fixed for the 10th. Jan· It is to be regretted that they could not be separated by a greater interval. I think we should bring our business forward early in January. The prints will be kept back till the Report is made. - I am very happy to hear from M^r. Garrett that the Proctor's accounts are satisfactorily settled . . . .

11. T.J., Monticello, to Joseph C. Cabell; Dec. 28, 1822; JP-1961; pp

. . . . Dinsmore's 70,000.D. evidence only the greediness of an Undertaker. he declined communicating the details of his estimate lest their exaggeration should be visible. from other undertakers we have the following offers.

	D	
the brickwork compleat including columns	11,300.	Perry
stone work	3,940.	Gorman
carpentry & joinery of the lower rooms	12,000·	Oldham
	27,240	

there remain the inside work of the upper room, the roof, & the two Appendages, or covered ways in the flanks to connect with the other buildings, of which we have no estimate but they cannot cost as much as all the rest of the building. I asked at what they had estimated the stone work? the answer was 6000.D. I knew at the same time that Gorman must do it for them, and would do it for 3,940.D. so that 50.p. was laid on this article for their gains, and probably like advances on the other articles. m^r Brockenbrough's original estimate was carefully and minutely made, and allowing for the two covered ways we are safe in saying that another loan of 60,000.D. will place us beyond the risk of ever needing to ask another Dollar on that account.

12. Arthur S. Brockenbrough, Contract with Dinsmore and Neilson; March 11, 1823; JP-1983 [Signed by Brockenbrough, Dinsmore and Neilson; witnessed by John M. Perry]

We, Arthur S. Brockenbrough Proctor acting for and in behalf of the University of Virginia on the one part, and James Dinsmore and John Neilson for themselves on the other part, do hereby enter into the following articles of agreement - Viz 1st A. S. Brockenbrough Proctor agrees that the said Dinsmore & Neilson may do the following parts of the Carpenters and Joiners work of the Rotunda Viz: All the Window frames & sashes, the two principal floors, the outside doors including the outside finishing, the staircases, all the centers for the brick work, the framing of the roof and sheeting, The portico framing & sheeting the Corinthian entablature all round complete - the Base & Cornice of the Attic, the Steping on the roof, the woodbucks and bond timbers &c that may be required hereafter for the finishing of the wood work, all to be executed in the best and most substantial manner - 2nd The materials for the above named work to be furnished at the expence of the University - 3rd The bills of Lumber to be made out by Dinsmore & Neilson and they to contract ·for the same on the best possible terms, to have the same well seasoned before it's used, to take care of the same and see that there is no unnecessary waste -

the Proctor to be furnished with a copy of all the bills of Lumber contracted for, as well as for bills of other articles that will be required for the said work 4th the brickwork to be laid off at the commencement by the said Dinsmore & Neilson and they are to examin the correctness of it as it progresses, and if not done agreeable to their direction to notify the Proctor in time for correction, but if any part of the brickwork done agreeable to the directions of the said Dinsmore & Neilson or either of them, should be found wrong, they the said Dinsmore & Neilson must pay for the necessary alteration of the brick work including the loss of materials & labour — 5th The prices of the aforesaid Carpenters work to be governed by the average prices of work in Philadelphia undertaken between the time of signing this contract and the completion of the work to be ascertained in the following manner. We are mutually to agree on two Philadelphia Measures to come on and measure the work, the prices shall be fixed agreeable to the present prices of work in Philadephia that is at the percentages above or below their price books, for all work not embraced in the said Books, they shall be guided by what they shall deem justice to both parties — 6th Money to be paid from time to time as the work progresses say Dollars per Month for each good hand employed on the said building including the undertakers - the Balance of the Bill at the completion of the work - each party to pay an equal proportion of the measuring charges - this contract to be null & void until approved by the Rector of the University of Virginia. Witness out hands and seals this 11th day of March One Thousand eight hundred & twenty three

13. T.J., Monticello, to Arthur S. Brockenbrough; March 12, 1823; JP-1983

I return you the contract with Dinsmore & Neilson which I approve of for the strong reasons assigned in your letter. I think my Colleagues, as well as myself are very desirous of being able at certain stages of the work to ascertain the exact state of our funds, that we may stop where they fail. the having to bring measures from Philadelphia may be some obstruction to that. but I presume we may hereafter find means of effecting that

I return you also the contract with Thorn & Chamberlain . · · .

14. T.J., Monticello, to Board of Visitors, UVa, Cabell's copy; March 12, 1823; JP-1984; pp

Having received from all our brethern approbations of the loan, I authorised Mr Brockenbrough to engage the work of the Rotunda, and have it commenced immediately. we had only two bricklayers and two carpenters capable of executing it with solidity and correctness; these had not capital enough for so great an undertaking, nor would they have risked their little all but for a great advance on the estimated cost, probably 50. percent. for this reason and others very decisive Mr Brockenbrough declined that mode of engagement, and on consideration of his reasons I approved of them. he has engaged Thorn and Chamberlain for the brickwork, and Dinsmore & Neilson for the roof and carpenter's work, on terms which I think will make our money go the farthest possible, for good work; and his engagement is only for the hull compleat. that done, we can pay for it, see the state of our funds and engage a portion of the inside-work so as to stop where our funds may fail, should they fail before it's entire completion. there it may rest ever so long, be used, and not delay the opening of the institution, the work will occupy three years. all this will be more fully explained at our meeting and will I hope receive your approbation . . . .

15. James Madison, Montpelier, to T.J.; March 21, 1823; (not in JP)

I have rec^d. your two letters of the 12. & 14. inst: You will have inferred my approbation of the course taken in order to avoid a loss of time in executing the Rotunda. I shall be with you at the Meeting of the Visitors if possible . . . .

16. T.J., Monticello, to Arthur S. Brockenbrough; April 22, 1823; JP-1993

Mr Dinsmore consulted me yesterday on the entablature of the Rotunda & of it's windows. I reviewed them, and find no reason to substitute any other than that of my original drawing for the main entablature, which was that of Palladio Book 1. Pl. 26. taking the base however from his plate 23. that of Pl. 25. having too much work as well as that of the Pantheon. I have examined carefully all the antient Corinthians in my possession, and observe that Palladio, as usual, has given the finest members of them all in the happiest combination.

I think too that his plates 35. 36. give the handsomest entablatures for windows that I can find anywhere, but I would adopt the architrave at the left hand bottom corner of pl. 35. give it a plain frize instead of his swelled one, and the dentil cornice at the bottom of pl. 36.

Will you be so good as to communicate this to Messrs Dinsmore & Neilson who I believe wait for them

17. John Neilson, University, to T.J.; May 5, 1823; JP-1997

I send you the north front of the Rotunda, by comparing it with the flank view, you will perceive a small difference in the North front the lower edge of the Architrave fills in the same line as the center of the Sphere. the column being then taken, leaves 10. ft. for the height of the Pedestal. if this be deemed too much which of the following modes would be agreeable to you to reduce it. First to raise the sphere in its cylinder, so as to shew a greater portion of the roof above the Steps, or it might be acomplished by adding to the height of the column. I believe you have objected to depressing the Sphere in the earth.

The scale I used for the Attic is 19.8 in. divided into 105' My anxiety to please, emboldens me to trouble you.

18. T.J., Monticello, to Arthur S. Brockenbrough; June 16, 1823; JP-2006

I mentioned to you yesterday the ill effect of the acute angles in the passage of the Rotunda. I send you my drawing of the building in which I have drawn portions of a circle to cover these angles. you will consider whether it is best to make them of brick or studs & laths. you will see in the drawing whereabouts the centers of those portions of circle are taken, so as to make the circle a tangent to the door post of the small room and side of the large one. be so good as to return my drawing . . . .

26

19. Joseph C. Cabell, Edgewood, to T.J.; July 18, 1823; JP-2012

    . . . . I am truly delighted to hear of the rapid progress of the Library . . . .

20. T.J., Monticello, to Arthur S. Brockenbrough; Aug. 10, 1823; JP-2017

I have but recently discovered that in my drawing of the Library room of the Rotunda, I have omitted to place a door in front, opening under the Portico, and I am happy in being in time to correct it. it should be of the width of the main door below, and it's soffite of the height of the soffites of it's coordinate windows. a folding sash door so as to give light when shut. it's bottom to be closed by an open pannel either Chinese or iron. it is not at all proposed however that there shall be any gallery to go out on, as that would injure the grandeur of the portico.

21. Arthur S. Brockenbrough, to T. J.; Aug. 11, 1823; JP-2019

Presuming you intended to have an opening in front over the main door below, I have had a stone sill & window frame prepared for it, which I think will answer better than a door, if however you prefer the door, it can be made. I should like to hear from you again on the subject.

22. T.J., Monticello, to Arthur S. Brockenbrough; Aug. 11, 1823; JP-2018

I think a door greatly preferable to a window both as to appearance & use. exactly such as in my parlour, except that the bottom pannels had better be of wood·

23. T.J., Monticello, to E. S. Davis; Aug. 27, 1823; JP-2020

    . . . . I now forward to you a plan of our University with printed explanations of it's several parts. these had not been prepared at the time you received the copy you posess. our Capitels from Italy are now rec^d. and in the course of a fortnight will all be up, and make the final finish of all our buildings of accomodation. the Rotunda for the Library & other purposes has it's walls raised to about 2/3 of their intended height, and thus will attain their full height in the course of another month. but the roof being weighty & from it's spherical form pressing outwardly in every direction we shall not venture it on our walls while green. it will not be put on therefore till the next summer, and the interior will require perhaps still another year. but the opening of the institution need not await that: and the general hope is that our legislature at their next session will remit the debt contracted under their authority by loans to the University from their Literary fund in this case the Visitors will require a twelve month to provide professors, because they mean to accept of none which are not of the 1st. order of science in their respective lines on whichever side of the Atlantic to be found . . . . our present accomodns are for 220. students but our plan admits enlargement as we find necessary . . . .

24. B of V, T.J.'s hand; Oct. 6, 1823; Report to the Literary Fund

. . . . in consequence hereof [drawing $ 40,000.00 from the Literary Fund] the larger buiding, for a library and other purposes was commenced & has been carried on with activity, inasmuch that its walls are now ready to receive their roof; but that being of hemispherical form, & pressing outwardly in every direction, it has been thought not advisable to place it on the walls, in their present green state; but rather to give them time to settle and dry until the ensuing season, when the roof will be ready, & the walls in a proper condition to receive it. whether the interior work of the building will be finished within the ensuing year, is doubtful . . . .

25. B. of V, Cabell's hand (?) ; Oct. 6, 1823

. . . . Resolved that they recommend to the executive committee to procure capitals of the same marble for the same columns if practicable on terms not higher than those offered by Thos. Appleton.

Resolved that they recommend also the said committee to procure squares of marble for paving the Portico of the Rotunda if they find that it can be done on terms preferable to what it will cost to have the same paved with country stone.

26. T.J., Monticello to Thomas Appleton; Oct. 8, 1823; JP-2029

. . . . The Visitors of the University had their meeting the day before yesterday, and I am now authorized to apply to you for the capitels of the columns of our Rotunda, agreeable to the following specifications.

Ten Corinthian capitels of marble for columns whose diminished diameters are 2 feet 8 4/10 inches English measure.

Two Corinthian semi-capitels for Pilasters, or halves of square columns of the same diminished diameter cut diagonally thus so as to present in front and flank each at the corners of the building. all to be copied exactly from those of the Pantheon, as represented by Palladio. B. 4. 20. pl. 60. Leoni's edition.

Our columns being of brick, in which no moulding can be worked it is necessary to subjoin to the capitel the astragal of the column making it a part of the same block. and the term astragal is meant to include (besides it's halfround member or Torus) the cavetto & listel below it, which meets the naked bock of the diminished shaft, and which will be seen in the same plate of Palladio's subjoined to the part B. of the capitel.

We have agreed with Giacomo Raggi for 10. bases and 2. diagonal pilaster bases for the same columns, according to the agreement inclosed. as he is not in circumstances sufficient to answer any failure of contract we have of necessity been obliged to ask your superintendance of his performance; and he places himself under your attentions as much as he would be under ours were we present. should you perceive any manifest intention on his part to abandon the performance, or any certain incompetence to the fulfilment, we will pray you to declare the contract disolved and to warn him to proceed no further. but if he goes on diligenty and hopefully we wish him to receive all reasonable indulgence. 50.D. have been advanced here to him on account. should he fail

28

in his contract, I will ask the favor of you to inform me without delay at what price we can get such bases furnished to us as our agreem^t specifies. this will determine us whether to get them here or there.

I will also ask the favor of you immediately on reciept of this to inform me at what price we can be furnished there with squares of marble to pave the floor of the portico of the Rotunda, polished and accurately squared ready to be laid down, the squares to be 1. foot square. we shall also have occasion in the interior of 40. composite capitels of *wood,* for columns whose diminished diameters are 15 11/16 Inches English, to be copied from Palladio B. 1. c. 18. pl. 30. What would they cost with you? I will thank you also for the best engraving of the Pantheon on a single sheet to be had with you.

This goes by Raggi and we this day desire Col^o. Bernard Peyton our Richmond correspondent to remit 4000.D. to you through Mr Williams of London, which is to include the payments to Raggi. the balance for the capitels according to the prices stated in your letter of July 7. 1821. shall be paid on delivery of them at Leghorn.

27. T.J., Monticello, to Arthur S. Brockenbrough; Nov. 22, 1823; JP-2034

Be pleased to place in the hands of Col^o. Bernard Peyton the sum of four thousand dollars to be invested by him in a bill of exchange to be remitted to Mr Appleton of Leghorn on account for the Capitels & bases of the columns of the Rotunda.

28. Arthur S. Brockenbrough, University, to T.J., March 28, 1824; JP-2061

Messrs. Dinsmore & Neilson without consulting with me have proceeded to purchase scantling and have framed the upper gallery floor of the library (altho' not embraced in the contract with them) and are now about to raise it; before they progress with it too far, I must beg permission to propose some alterations that has struck my mind on seeing the hight of the gallery and which I think will be an improvement — The Circumference of the Library room is about 229 feet the height of the wall to the spring of the arch about 18 ft which gives us more than 4000 superficial feet (including the openings) for book cases without going to the upper Gallery which comes immediately under the roof for another set of cases, and in which case you would conceal a part of the cieling very much to the injury of the look of the room particularly if the cieling should be enriched with sunken pannel work to — In the place of the two Galleries I should prefer one on Column about ten feet high the entablature to be above the floor in that case your lower cases would be about ten feet high which could easily come at the upper cases about seven feet — The Columns will be smaller and consequently less expensive & one entire Gallery will be saved there by — if the weather should be fit they (D & N) will be raising the floor tomorrow. if you wish time to consider on it, you can direct that part of the business to be delayed awhile — I hope you will pardon me for thus making known my thoughts on this subject when I assure you it is done with a good motive

[endorsed, as follows, in T.J.'s hand:]

disapproved

29. T.J., Monticello, to Arthur S. Brockenbrough; March 29, 1824; JP-2062

I have considered maturely the change you propose in the library, and see no advantage in altering the original plan. in that, besides the 4000 feet for presses below the entablature of the columns, we can have another tier of presses above the entablature, of one half more of the space. again instead of the noble perystyle of the original nearing a proper proportion to the height of vault above, it proposes a diminutive one of 10.f. height with a vault of 40.f. above. the original peristyle by it's height & projection from the wall has the advantage of hiding a portion of the vault of which too much would otherwise be seen. the panneled plaistering makes no difficultie because it will be divided by cross styles into compartments, and thus adapted to the view. Messrs. Nelson & Dinsmore should be warned that if they do any thing more than what was proposed to be first done, there will be no funds to pay for it.

30. Arthur S. Brockenbrough, University, to T.J.; April 5, 1824; JP-2066

An Estimate of the cost of the Rounda as far as the contracts that have been made towards the completion of it go —

Amt. paid for Materials for the brickwork	$ 6905.47	
' p to Thorn & Chamberlain for the work	2856.25	9,761.72
' To complete the brickwork of the Library & Terras say		1,000.00
Amt. Contract with G. Raggi for 10 Bases & 2 Pilaster bases	715.00	
Cost of Capitels in Italy say	7000.00	
Transportation, duty &c. on the same & bases	2450.00	10,165.00
pd for Stone Window & doorsills	255.00	
to complete the stone steps on the back & Terras Stone work	1200.00	1,455.00
paid for Materials principally Lumber & iron which nearly pays for all the Lumber		6,165.00
For Tin & Copper for the roof of Dome & Portico		2,000.00
Glass & Glazing including the skylight		500.00
		$ 31,046.72

Nails, hardware, painting & Workman's bills will not I presume exceed the balance of the $ 41,000

31. T.J., Monticello, to Thomas Appleton; May 17, 1824; JP-2081

My last to you was of Nov. 22. since which I have received yours of Dec. 24. and Feb. 8. in consequence of the information given in the last that the first quality of marble squares for paving the Portico of our Rotunda, polished and accurately squared ready to be laid down, of one foot square, will cost at

Leghorn 22½ D. the hundred I am now to desire you to send us 1400 squares of one foot each . . . .

P.S. will safety require the marble squares to be secured in packages? if it does, they must be secured.

32. Arthur S. Brockenbrough, University, to T.J.; June 4, 1824; JP-2085

Messrs Thorn & Chamberlain are about to commence the brick work of the Attic of the Rotunda, would it not be advisable to put reservoirs in the two North corners of the Rotunda by arching over the present openings and then by masking the reservoirs nearly the depth of the attic and as large in diameter as the Space will admit of, the water from thence may be thrown (in case of fire) to any part of the building below the Dome by pipes. be pleased to let me know what you think of the plan in the morning as the delay of a day will probably make some difference . . . .

33. Arthur S. Brockenbrough, University, to T.J.; July 14, 1824; JP-2090

As Mr Gorman is about to commence with the back steps of the Rotunda it is necessary that the plan should be positively fixed on. I therefore wish to know your wishes on the subject. I have layed down several plans if you approve of any one of them mark the one you like best or send a plan that you like better than any one of them — If the earth is removed from steps, it will make the flight 18 feet high, the present arch must necessarily come down and the flight run out 4 or 6 feet beyond the corner of the building, where we have nothing but made earth for 6 or 8 feet deep — Agreeable to Plan A a part of the circle only would require facing and coping with stone from point E to the Gymnasia — Plan B all the ruff work would be concealed by the fall — Queri, would you prefer the out side wall of the steps sloped as plan A, or square up to the platform as Plan B - ? 20 feet for a platform, I think little enough, nor will it do to encroach more on the arch than is layed down in the several plans . . . .

34. William J. Coffee, New York, to T.J.; Sept. 11, 1824; LC

. . . . can't say at the moment the time you may expect the ornaments however I will say for your satisfaction that no other business shall Interrupt your roses, till the number is Complete.

One thing I consider necessary for me to know, which Information your letter does not give, it is the distance these Ornaments are to be seen, as you are well acquainted that the effect will depend on the Boldness of the floor which must be ruled by a Knowledge of the Hight the roses will be Placed. Should you not have time perhaps M^r. Brockinbro will give me that Immediate Information. in the mean time I Shall make every Necessary preparation.

[The following notes are in T.J.'s hand:]

	f
basement	8
from floor of portico to soffite of frize	33

35. B of V; Oct. 4, 1824

. . . . The upper circular room of the Rotunda shall be reserved for a Library.

One of it's larger rooms on it's middle floor shall be used for annual examinations, for lectures for such schools as are too numerous for their ordinary schoolrooms, & for religious worship under the regulations allowed to be prescribed by law: the other rooms on the same floor may be used by schools of instruction in drawing, music, or any other of the innocent and ornamental accomplishments of life; but under such instructors as shall be approved and licenced by the Faculty. The rooms in the Basement story of the Rotunda shall be, one of them for a Chemical laboratory; and the others for any necessary purpose for which they may be adapted.

The two open apartments adjacent to the same story of the Rotunda shall be appropriated to the Gymnastic exercises and games of the Students, among which shall be reckoned military exercises . . . .
Resolved that it is the opinion of the board that if the arrearages of subscriptions should not be sufficient to pay for the articles of marble contracted for in Italy, it will be proper to supply the deficiency from the annuity of the year 1825.

36. B of V, T.J.'s hand; Oct. 5, 1824; Report to the Literary Fund

. . . . in the course of the present season this building [the Rotunda] has received it's roof, and will be put into a condition for preservation and use, although it's interior cannot be compleated . . . .

37. T.J., Monticello, to Francis Walker Gilmer; Oct. 12, 1824; JP-2100

. . . . . he [Gen. Lafayette] is to visit Montpellier and Monticello within about 3 weeks, and to accept a public dinner in our University. the Rotunda is sufficiently advanced to receive him . . . .

38. Clipping from the PORTSMOUTH (N.H.?) JOURNAL; Nov. 24, 1824; JP-2104

. . . . If, with the aid of my younger and abler co-adjutors, I can still contribute anything to advance the institution, within whose walls we are now mingling manifestations to this our guest, it will be, as it has ever been, cheerfully and zealously bestowed . . . .

39. T.J., Monticello, to William J. Coffee; Dec. 9, 1824; LC

When shall we get our roses for the Rotunda? the whole scaffolding of the building is obliged to be kept standing only to enable the workmen to put up these small ornaments. I am sure you have been using due diligence, yet our necessity obliges us to make this enquiry. our inst^n will certainly be opened on the 1st. of Feb, and the Rotunda will be then in a cond^n for use . . . .

40. William J. Coffee, New York, to T.J.; Dec. 20, 1824; LC

Sir you wish to know when you are to have the ornaments for the Rotunda; I answer that they are all finished, and only wait the Packing and Enshipment, to be on the way for their institution.

no time shall be lost on my part to get them under way and then the risks of the seas must be yours the Last was mine and I insured them.

I do not see any necessary directions to your People onless it is to say I think it will be proper to use round headed Screws for the purpose of Puting them into a kind of Lock Screw.

my reason is the less likely hood of Spliting the Rose otherwise used the heads must be filed off on the sides

They are Very hard and will be found to last as long as any part of the Building this much I may Venture to say in their behalf. Your order was for 330 wanted and 15 over to meet chances I have made 350 but shall Pack 355 to meet any small Loss by Conveyors which I do not fear as I shall take the same [illegible word] of Packing as before. in a few day I shall do myself the Pleasure of writing to you again Inclosing to you and to Mr. Brockenbro Bill of Lading.

41. Arthur S. Brockenbrough, University, to T.J.; Dec. 21, 1824; JP-2110

Measurement of the Dome from the top of the last step to the center of the Sky light 27 feet 5 inches.
Dr Sir

Above you have the measurement of dome of the Rotunda above the steps - . . . .

42. William J. Coffee, New York, to T.J.; Jan. 1, 1825; LC

To Prommis I have shipped the ornaments and have inclosed an extra Bill of Lading for Mr. A. S. Brockenbrogs so that directions may be sent to the consigne to forward them according to your wish to the University.

The Scooner whent to seae on the 29 and as the wether has been unusually fine should conclude she may have reached her distined Port by the time you get this Information. this same paper contains the account which I hope will meet with your Approbation. and If I can receive it in the following way it will answer my Purpose.

To say I shall be glad to receve from the Proctor as Promptly as Possible the sum of $ 45 it may be sent me in cash Inclosed at the Proctor's [illegible word], or, by a Bill at Sight on Richmond, considering at the time that the Exchange is in favour of New York one and 2/3 pr cent. The remaining Ballancs I shall not want till the first of May . . . .

43. T.J., Monticello, to Joseph C. Cabell; Jan 11, 1825; JP-2131; pp

. . . . it will take about 25.M.D. more than we have to finish the Rotunda . . . .

44. William J. Coffee, New York, to T.J.; Jan. 16, 1825; LC

That no time might be lost I called on Mr Maverick the same day I recived your favour dated the 5. Jany. which came to hand not till the 14th. I

stated to him your wishes and the following is his answer Viz that owing to
Ill health his business has out of necessity being neglected that now they are
in hand and will Positively be forwarded to Richmond from this City in the
whole of the following Week.

In reply to your note on the want of the roses I can only say they was
Shiped on the 27th. of last December, and that the Scooner whent to sea on
the 29. Information was rendered to the Consigne on the 28. and on the 2 of
Jany 25. An Extra Bill of Lading was forwarded to your care for Mr. A. S.
Brockingbrou. with *that* a letter of advices to you to the same tenor. Those
letters I have no doubt have reached your hand before this time and most
probably the ornaments. Information of which I hope to be favoured with
from Mr. Brockingbrou on the arrival of Ornaments . . . .

45. T.J., Monticello, to Joseph C. Cabell; Jan. 19, 1825; JP-2139; pp

. . . . in the meantime Mr Brockenbrough is in the utmost distress for about
5000.D. due on acct of the Rotunda . . . .

46. B of V, T.J.'s hand; March 5, 1825

. . . . Resolved that on payment of the sd sum of 50.M.D. by the General
government a sum not exceeding 6000.D. thereof be advanced on loan to
the building fund of the University for the purpose of finishing the interior
of the library room . . . .

47. T.J., Monticello, to Alexander Garrett; March 8, 1825; JP-2157

. . . . We should immediately, and without any delay remit the sum of 3000.D
to Mr Appleton on account of our capitels, bases and pavement. the proper
channel will be for Colo. Peyton to purchase a bill on London payable to Mr
Saml. Williams No. 13. Finsbury square London to the credit of Thomas Appleton Consul of the US. at Leghorn, with a request to remit it to him on account
of the University of Virginia; inclosing with it to Mr Williams a letter of advice
addressed to Mr Appleton. it should go by duplicates, and the bill should be
of such an amount as to place the nett sum of 300.D. clear of exchange in
London.

48. T.J., Monticello, to Arthur S. Brockenbrough; March 9, 1825; JP-2158

I omitted in my letter of this morning, to desire you to have remitted immediately to mr Appleton the sum of 3000.D. towards payment for our capitels, paviment,
and the bases which Raggi has agreed to furnish, but is not able to do it. in
a letter to mr Garrett I have pointed out the course of effecting it through Colo
Peyton.

49. William J. Coffee, New York, to T.J.; March 21, 1825; LC

. . . . I am under the necessity of Asking the favour of you to beg Mr. Brockinbro
to forward me the Ballances Due, on or about the 20th of April . . . .

50. Thomas Appleton, Leghorn, Account to T.J.; May 4, 1825; JP-2175; Stamped and signed by Jonathan Thompson, Collector, of New York

Thomas Jefferson esq. of Monticello to Thomas Appleton of Leghorn—Dr TJ

No. 1 to 19 To 19 cases containing 1400 marble squares for paving @ 22½ Dollars the hundred	)))	Dollars	315 —
No. 20 - 31 To 12 cases containing ten whole & two half marble bases for columns	))		866.
		Dollars	1181

Charges

To 31 cases @ £ 7 each £ 217	£ 217		
To custom house duties @ £ 2	62.—		
To cartage & porterage to Ship	52.—		
	£331 @ £ 6 ⅓		52.25
	Dollars		1233.25

Dr.   Thomas Jefferson esq. in Account current with Thomas Appleton

1825 To amt. of the within account of Sculptured marble works	Dollars 1233.25	1823 April By Bale due you as by account rendered at this	Dollars
To Bale due you carried to the credit of the Capitals	2875.50	1824 Jany Date By 3 Bills of Excha from Samuel Williams of London, which after deducting various postages to do. & postages pd. by me &c. Discount here, as they were at 3 mos Returned	189.75
			3919 —
Dollars	4108.75	Spanish Dollars	4108.75.

1825
4 May By Bala brought from above

Dollars Cts.
2875.50

51. Arthur S. Brockenbrough, University, to T.J.; June 6, 1825; JP-2192

In finishing the Library room of the Rotunda in what way do you propose securing it at the head of the stairs? whether by a partition around the well hole of the Stairs and a door in the front of landing or a lobby extending to the rear of the columns next the Stairs? I should be glad to have your opinion on the subject. - Dr Emmet I find is much dissatisfied with the proposed arrangement for his laboratory — He thinks the small room in the basement of the Rotunda will not answer the purpose for the want of room & light — He wishes to have the use of both of the large oval rooms in the basement one for his lecture room the other for a laboratory. if this be granted him where then shall the room for a Museum be fited up? — Will the dining room of the Pavilion N°. 1 answer that purpose for the present? — or the rooms on the 2nd floor of the same pavilion? . . . .

52. T.J., Monticello, to Arthur S. Brockenbrough; June 7, 1825; JP-2184

. . . . Dr. Emmet can have both the large basement rooms & to be arranged as he pleases for his chemical purposes. in that case we will use one of the upper oval rooms for a museum. The wells of the staircases are to be secured by a ballustrade, for which, as well as the staircases I send you a very beautiful form of balluster. it will [illegible word] be weeks yet before I shall be able to visit the University, even in a carriage . . . .

53. Arthur S. Brockenbrough, University, to T.J.; June 9, 1825; JP-2195

I find by your favor of the 7th I did not express myself in a way to be unstood by you relative to the finish at the head of the stairs of the Rotunda - Without a partition at the head of the stairs any person entering the building will have free access to the Library - there is nothing to prevent it from the Basement to the library room - as the lower part of the building will be in use, consequently open, I do suppose something will be necessary to prevent any & every person from Entering except with the Librarian

54. Thomas Appleton, Leghorn, Account to T.J.; July 12, 1825; JP-2212

Thomas Jefferson esq. of Virg^a to Thomas Appleton of Leghorn - D^r.

1825			Dollars
June	To amount of 10 whole & half Capitals as p account rendered		6270.27

Credit

1825		Doll.	
May	By balance due in account of May	2875.50	
July	By a bill of exchange remitted me, by Saml. Williams of London, which bill is due 28. Sept. & when paid will produce	3032.—	
		5907.50	
Balance due Thomas Appleton		362.77	6270.27

55. T.J., Monticello, to Arthur S. Brockenbrough; July 23, 1825; JP-2214

Th. Jefferson asks the favor of mr Brockenbrough to inform him of the date of the remittance of 3000.D to mr Appleton this last spring. everything from him may be daily expected. all, except the capitels were on board ship at the date of his letter Apr 13. everything should therefore be got in rediness to run up the columns immediately. send me also Raggi's contract for the bases.

56. T.J., Monticello, to Arthur S. Brockenbrough; July 24, 1825; JP-2216

. . . . The marble bases and paving squares will come in the ship Caroline Capt. Farmer, for N. Y. he was to sail the last of April from Leghorn. the Capitels would be shipped in May. I return you Raggi's agreem^t.

57. T.J., Monticello, to Thomas Appleton; Aug. 10, 1825; JP-2222

I had been so long without hearing from you (my last from you being dated Oct. 8. 24.) that I sat down to communicate my anxieties to you which I had actually done in a long letter when the mail of that day brought me yours of Apr. 13. and rendered mine of course useless. I learnt with regret that you had suffered inconvenience from the want of remittances. your former letters had given me reason to believe that the last and most important articles of our marble works would be ready for delivery in May.
on the 7th. of Mar. therefore I had had a remittance made of the sum of 3000.D. which you suppose would be about the balance due to you, and which would reach you in May in readiness for the delivery. the following statem^t. of payments is I believe nearly exact.

			D.
1823.	Oct. 6.	we ordered 10. Corinth^n. Capitels for a dim^d diam. of 32.4 (I.Eng.) @ 550 (D)	5500
		2. semi-capitels for pilasters @ 290. (D) each	580
		cases, say about	60
1824.	May 17.	we ordered 1400. sq. ft. paving slabs @ 22½ (d) p^r. 100. feet	315
			6455
1823.	Oct. 8.	we remitted 4000.D. which netted 3,940.50	
1825.	Mar. 7.	we remitted 3000. (D) netting perhaps not quite 3,000	6940.50
		making a balance in that account in our favor of ab^t	485.50
		cash advanced to Raggi	50.
			535.50
1823.	Sept. 8.	Raggi's contract for 10. bases to the columns @ 65 = 650 (D)	
		2. semibases @ 32.50 65) 715	
suppose an additional allowance		100	815.

balance due T.A. for capitels, bases, pavement   280.50
This Apercu would make a balance still due you from the University of 280. D. which should be now remitted were it the exact one. but hoping you will have sent an exact one with the Capitels &c I shall defer remitting till I recieve the

exact one when a remittance of the exact balance will inclose the present transactions between the University and yourself.

58. William J. Coffee, New York, to T.J.; Aug. 19, 1825; LC

Some time ago, M^r. Antrim the Plasterer for the University, called on me with Drawings for ornaments to decorate the in Side of the Rotundo, and requested that I would State to M^r. Brockingbrou the terms on which I would execute. this I did in as Plain a Manner as I could but owing to *Something* I have not recived any reply to those terms so long sent in, or to a letter sins sent to M^r. Brockingbrou on the same subject, as I have other Business that I must Immediately attend to or decline according as the decision may be be in regard to the ornaments for the University, beg that I may be permited to ask you Sir whether the ornaments will be wanted - and if wanted at wat time . . . .

59. T.J., Monticello, to Ellen Wayles Randolph Coolidge; Aug. 27, 1825; JP-2227; pp

. . . . I am expecting to hear from Mr. Coolidge on the subject of the clock for the Rotunda . . . .

60. T.J., Monticello, to Arthur S. Brockenbrough; Aug. 30, 1825; JP-2229

The marble bases and paving squares are arrived at N. Y. and will be immediately reimbarked thence for Richm^d.

T.I.

Cases N°. 1 - to 19. contain 1400. sq.f. of paving squares, and 12. other cases N°. 20. to 31 contain 10. whole and 2 half bases for the columns. as their transportation from Richmond up will be extremely difficult and expensive, special measures should be provided for it. the stone alone will weigh 30. tons besides the cases which are strong and heavy. cases 20 to 31. should be brought first, if all do not come together, because they contain the bases, and will enable us instantly on their arrival to begin the columns. I am obliged to send the invoice to the Collector of New York that he may ascertain duties, freight and other charges to be remitted to him immediately . . . .

The Capitels were on their way from Carrara to Leghorn to be embarked on another vessel then in that port for N. York.

61. Henry A. S. Dearborn, Boston, to T.J.; Sept. 6, 1825; JP-2232

By the Brig Tamworth just arrived from Leghorn, I received a letter from Mr. Appleton Esqr. U. S. Consul, & a bill of lading of twenty four cases of marble capitals, Charlottesville, made by your order.

I shall ship them by the first vessel bound to Richmond, to the care of Col. B. Peyton & will inform him by mail of the name of the vessel & time she will leave this port.

Mr. Appleton informs me that they must be moved with care, although nicely packed, in strong boxes. He says they will be found, probably inferior in dimensions, but certainly equal in architectural perfection, to any in the U.S., & that they were copied from those of the Pantheon at Rome. I will see that they are tranship & with care & give notice to Col. Peyton to cause the boxes to be handled with great caution.

[the following is a notation in T.J.'s hand:]

1823. Oct. 8. Capitels were ordered. duty then 15. p.c.
1824. May 22. date of new Tariff law on marble & manufact^{re}. of d^o. 30. p.c. ad. val

62. Jonathan Thompson, New York, to T. J.; Sept. 9, 1825; JP-2233

I received your letter of the 30th ultimo. with two Invoices enclosed, for the Marble by the Ship Caroline from Leghorn. The Invoices are returned herewith agreeably to your request. The marks do not agree with the Invoices & bill of lading received. I have entered the Marble and paid the duty thereon copies of the entries are enclosed, & have shipped the same on board the Sloop Eliza Allen, Capt. Allen for Richmond consigned to Col. Bernard Peyton as per bills of lading herewith transmitted. The freight from Leghorn have paid, amounting to three hundred and thirty dollars, as per bills also herewith.

Duties on 31 Cases	$ 394.32
d^o 6 d^o	61.19
	455.51
Freight from Leghorn	330.—
Doll^s.	785.51

[the following is a notation in T.J.'s hand:]

note. for the 6. cases of Th:J he remitted	
for duties	61.19
for freight	66.
	127.19
leaving to be remitted for the 31. cases	
of Univ. by A. S. B.	658.32
	785.51

63. T.J., Monticello, to Arthur S. Brockenbrough; Sept. 13, 1825; JP-2235

The capitels are arrived at Boston and now on their way to Richm^d. The balance due to mr Appleton is 362.77 which should be promptly paid and he permits to be paid in Boston: the duties at New York & Boston I suppose will be about 1200.D. to be also promptly payable. the cases with the capitels are so heavy that 2. different ships at Leghorn refused to take them.

64. T.J., Monticello, to Henry A. S. Dearborn; Sept. 13, 1825; JP-2236; pp

I recieved yesterday your favor of the 6th. and supposing it possible that m^r Appleton may not have sent you an invoice of the cost of the marble for our University arrived in your port, so as to enable you to settle the duties I inclose you his account furnished to me, by which you will see what their prime cost has been. these marble capitels were ordered Oct. 8, 1823. the new Tariff law was not passed till May 22. 24. retrospective laws are so professedly unjust that we propose to petition Congress for a remission of the additional duties. those existing when we ordered the articles we will pay immediately [illegible word], I hope, Sir, it may be in your power so to arrange the demand, as to suspend the actual call for the additional part until we have an opportunity of applying to Congress. the marbles you have recieved, and others arrived at N. York would subject the University to about 1200.D. additional to what existed when they were ordered. I pray a return of the inclosed paper . . . .

65. T.J., Monticello, to Thomas Voight; Sept. 21, 1825; JP-2238

The University of Virgi lately built with which I am connected will have occasion for a large clock and bell, such an one as may be heard 2. miles distinctly and habitually. are such made in Philadelphia, and what would be the separate price of the clock and bell? we wish works substantially good.

In the mean time I shall request you to send us an 8. day clock in a mahogany case neat, without expensive ornaments, but of excellent workmanship and a loud bell. first however inform me what the price of such an one will be and how soon it can be furnished and suspend any thing more till I answer you. we need it with as little delay as possible.

66. Henry A. S. Dearborn, Boston, to T.J.; Sept. 22, 1825; JP-2239

Your letter of the 13th was recieved yesterday.—As you are entitled to a credit of eight, ten & twelve months, for the duties, a third of the amount becoming due at the expiration of those periods, from the time of importation, it will be the better way to give bonds accordingly, which will afford you the opportunity of petitioning Congress before either bond is to be paid, for the remission of a part & I think you should have of the whole of the duties: for the same principal which actuated, in exempting Books, Philosophical Apparatus, Specimens of Sculpture &c. &c. &c. from duty, when imported for any Seminary of learning, should govern in relation to these Capitals, which, while they are to embelish the University, present superb models of antient Architecture, & I trust a liberal Spirit will induce the National Legislature to exonerate you from the payment of the bonds. This *indirect* aid they should, *at least,* afford for the encouragement of learning. — Presuming that it might be possible you would giving one bond, for the whole duties, which will be for Eight months, instead of dividing the amount into three bonds which you have a right to do, I have sent such a bond marked A & if you conclude to sign that, the Three others may be destroyed, but if the whole period of credit is desired, please to execute the three marked B. C. & D. and add two names as Sureties. The entry you will be so good as to Sign & Swear to it, before a Magistrate, and return it to me with the bonds executed.—

Below is a Statement of the insurance I have effected & a minute of the expensis I have paid, or shall pay when the Capitals have reached Richmond, also the Amount of duties.

Amount Insured made up of the following items.

Cost of 24 cases Marble at Leghorn as per Invoice	$ 6233.78
Freight from Leghorn to Boston	795.30
Wharfage &c.	17.50
Duties at Boston	2057.15
	$ 9103.73

40

Amount Insured at Merchants Office Boston   4552.00
      Do   Franklin   Do   Do   4552.00

Premium of Insurance due each Office is $ 34.14
rate at 3 or 4 month^s Credit.
Expenses which I have paid or Shall pay.
1. Freight from Leghorn $ 795.30
2. Wharfage &c   17.50
3. Amount premium & policies   72.58 $ 885.08

                 Impost on Marble at Boston   2057.15

                                    $.2942.23

I am sorry to give you so much trouble and would avoid it all, if it were in my power.——
H. A. S. Dearborn Esq to Henry Hovey & Co Dr.

Sept. 1825   For sundry expenses on 24 Boxes Marble
             for Brig Tamworth from Leghorn — viz.
             Paid Wharfage the above as pr Bluney's bill $ 5.00
             Paid extra labour on the above   2.50
             advertising &c. for a vessel to freight
             the above to Richmond   10.00

                                       17.50

Boston September 20th. 1825
Rc^d Payment
Henry Hovey & Co

Policy No. 1816   Boston, September 22. 1825
For Value Received, I promise to pay the Franklin Insurance Company, or Order, in Four months from the date, with interest after, the sum of Thirty-five 14/100 dollars ——
Prem. 34.14   H A S Dearborn
Pol.   1.   by Nath. Tracy

    35.14

67. Arthur S. Brockenbrough, University, to T. J.; Oct. 1, 1825; JP-2240

You will see from the within, I have brought Mr W. J. Coffee down in his charges for his composition ornaments 50 p^r cent. I submit it to your Consideration whether it would be prudent or not in the present low state of our finances to order on those ornaments even at this reduced price
P.S. I shall attend to your letter of to day & send you the statement tomorrow

[Enclosure in JP-2240; William J. Coffee, New York, to Arthur S. Brockenbrough; Aug. 25, 1825.]

Your obliging favour of the 10th of this month, is now before me. I attentively notice the whole of it's contents and reply as follows
For reasons stated in my last, and as Circumstances now stand, I agree to

furnish the Ornaments for the frize allso the Leaves for the Modillions and the rosetts, on *your own terms,* that is 50 pr. Cent —— below the first Prices, exclusive of the Charges attending on the Packing, Packing Cases, Paper Carting and Shiping. ————————————————

I now State the Manu I agree to execuit those Ornaments the whole of the frize (except a very small Part of the *small* Parts) will be in my Burnt Composition.

The Leaves of the Modillions will be made in thin Lead.

The Rosetts will be all Made in my Burnt Composition.

The payment I should require as soon as you are Properly Noticed by the Capt\[s\]. Bills of Lading - $ 70 - the remaining sum in the Middle of April 1826 say 15 —— free of all expenses of Exchange —— but it will be necessary for me to have the order compleat —— by the 12 of October on accnt of having sufficient time to compleat the work (which will take over three Months) by the Month of February for on the first of March I shall be in Washington, and on the first of May I have engaged to execuit on the Spot some Large Roman Cement Ornaments, at the Collegiate Church now Building in Canada.

68. Jonathan Thompson, New York, to T.J.; Oct. 3, 1825; JP-2242

Your letter of the 13th. ult. I have received, previous to which I had paid the duties on the Marble received by the Ship Caroline for the University of Virginia, and for yourself, forwarded the accounts to you by Mail. I have this day received a letter from Col. B Peyton, with a check for One hundred & twenty seven dollars, and nineteen cents, being the amount of Duties & Charges on *your six* cases of marble mantles.

69. B. of V, T.J.'s hand; Oct. 5, 1825

. . . . The act of Congress imposing an additional duty of 15. per cent on works of marble having been past after the marble capitels for the Portico of the Rotunda had been ordered, it is considered as retrospective and unjust, and that it will be proper to apply to Congress for a remission of that portion of duty thereon, and as it may be thought by that body but a just encouragement to science to relieve the University from the old as well as new duties on the marbles recently received for the same building, it will be expedient to bond the whole duties for 8. months to give time for application to Congress on the subject.

And thereupon the members executed the requisite bond in their individual characters, instructing at the same time the Proctor to retain in his hands always a sufficient sum to pay the duties old and new if ultimately required . . . .

70. B. of V, T.J.'s hand; Oct. 7, 1825

. . . . The last report stated that in addition to the sum of 19,370.40½ D which had been paid or provided towards the building called the Rotunda, there were still remaining, of the general funds, a sum of about 21,000.D. applicable to this building. that this sum, altho not sufficient to finish it, would put it into a state of safety and of some uses, until other and more pressing objects should have been accomplished. it has been indispensable to finish the circular room destined for the reception of the books; because, once deposited in their places, the removing them, for any finishing which might be left to be done hereafter, would be inadmissible, that has therefore been carried on actively, and we trust will be ready in time for the reception of the books. the other apartments of indispensable use were, two for a Chemical laboratory, one for a Museum of Natural history, and one for Examinations, for accessory schools, and other associated purposes. an additional building too for Anatomical dissections, and other kindred uses, was become necessary. we are endeavoring to put these into a bare state for use, altho' with some jeapardy as to the competence of the funds . . . .

71. T.J., Monticello, to Arthur S. Brockenbrough; Oct. 9, 1825; JP-2246

Genl. Dearborn, Collector of Boston, has advanced the expences on our marble Capitels as follows

Freight from Leghorn	795.30
Warfage Etc.	17.50
Amount premium and policies	72.28
	885.08

which advance being gratuitous and an uncommon favor be pleased to have him reimbursed without any delay.

72. T.J., Monticello, to Arthur S. Brockenbrough; Oct. 12, 1825; JP-2248

Mr. Brockenbrough was before desired to remit to Genl. Dearborne Collector of Boston on the marble capitels arrived there

Freight from Leghorn to Boston	795.30
Expenses in Boston	17.50
Insurance	72.28
	885.08

[Note in ASB's hand: "Nov 9 25 Voucher ?"]

he is now desired to remit to Jonathan Thompson, Collector of New York on the bases & pavement arrived there

Duties on 31. cases @ 30. p.c.	394.32
Freight from Leghorn to N. York	264 -
	658.32

[Note in ASB's hand: "Check remitd to Nickd Nov: 10 '25"]

D c

. . . . there remains due to Thos. Appleton 362.77 to be remitted to Thos. Perkins, President of the Union insurance, Boston

[Note in ASB's hand: "check remitted to Nickd Nov 10 '25"]

73. T.J., Monticello, to Joseph Coolidge, Jr.; Oct. 13, 1825; JP-2250; pp

. . . . the information particularly which you were so kind as to obtain and furnish me, as to the cost of a college clock should have been answered, but finding the price you mentioned far beyond our expectations and funds, I took time to have other enquiries made. these however did not reˢult in bringing the cost more within our means. on the contrary, 40. cents the M were asked for a bell in Philadelphia, instead of .35. the price with you. we are obliged therefore to do without until our funds are improved; and this ought to have been said to you sooner.

74. Henry A. S. Dearborn, Boston, to T.J.; Oct. 21, 1825; JP-2253

Your letter of the 13ᵗʰ inst. enclosing the bond &c., has been recᵈ., also one from John Brockenbrough Esq of Richmond enclosing a Draft on the New England Bank in this city for 885. 8 Dollars which has been paid.
                                                                                        ——
                                                                                        100
On paying the premium for insurance I find that the charges for the policies were included in them, & therefore return you the two dollars, in a Draft from the New England Bank, on the Farmer's Bank in Richmond. — I enclose the following named vouchers for the Sums charged you. —

Nᵒ. I Ropes Reed & Co. Freight bill	$ 759.30
Nᵒ. 2 Henry Hovey's bill	17.50
' 3)	
4) Policies & premium notes paid	70.28
5)	
6)	
	————
	883.08
Draft on Farmers Bank in your favor	2.00
	————
Dollˢ.	885.08

I am very happy to hear the capitals reached Richmond in Safety, & hope some day, to have the pleasure of beholding them surmounting their Columns. ——

75. T.J., Monticello, to Arthur S. Brockenbrough; Nov. 12, 1825; JP-2258

. . . . I send you a letter of Mʳ Samuel Williams of London which as a voucher for monies remitted thro' him to Appleton, should be placed among your files . . . .

76. T.J., Monticello, to Ellen Wayles Randolph Coolidge; Nov. 14-26, 1825; JP-2259; pp

. . . . I remark what you say in your letter to your mother relative to mr Willard and our University clock. judging from that that he is the person whom mr Coolidge would recommend, and having received from Dʳ. Watterhouse a very strong recommendation of him, you may assure the old gentleman from me that he shall have the making of it. we have lately made an important purchase of lands amounting to 7000.D. and the Government is taking from us, under their old and new Tariff, 2700.D. duty on the marble caps and bases of the Portico of our Rotunda, of 10 columns only. these things try our funds for the moment. at the end of the year we shall see how we stand, and I expect we may be able to give the final order for the clock by February . . . .

77. T.J., Monticello, to Arthur S. Brockenbrough; Nov. 15, 1825; JP-2260

. . . . I inclose you a letter from the Collector of N. York shewing that he has not yet recieved the 638.32 for freight and duties on the marble landed there. I find by my letter to him of Oct. 11. that I informed him I had that day desired you to remit that sum to him immediately. will you enquire into this and let me know what excuse I may make to him. these gentlement are so obliging in their advances of freight and duty for us, that we should be very prompt in replacing their advances. I shall not answer him until I hear from you . . . .

78. Jonathan Thompson, New York, to T.J.; Nov. 17, 1825; JP-2261

By the Mail of this day I recd a check from the Cashier of the Bank of Virginia for six hundred & fifty eight Dollars & $\frac{32}{100}$ being a remittance by request of the Proctor of the University of Virginia & in full for the balance due me for duties & freight of Marble . . . .

79. T.J., Monticello, to Arthur S. Brockenbrough; Jan. 3, 1826; JP-2273

The temporary bell should be placed on the ridge of the roof of the Pavilion in which the books now are, on a small gallows exactly as the tavern bells are. you will contrive how the cord may be protected from the ticklish ringings of the students. when the clock comes from Richmond, it should be placed before a window of the book room of the same house, the face so near the window as that it's time may be read thro' the window from the outside . . . . it is high time to have our bookcases in hand, and to be pressed as the books cannot be opened until the shelves are ready to recieve them. the boxes from France, lately shipped from N. York must be now arrived at Richmond.

80. T.J., Monticello, to Joseph C. Cabell; Feb. 4, 1826; JP-2286; pp

. . . . The arresting all avoidable expence is the more necessary as our application to Congress for a remission of duties (3000.D.) has past the committee of claims by a majority of a single vote only, and has still a long gauntlet to run . . . .

81. William C. Rives, Washington, to T.J.; March 13, 1826; JP-2298

I had the pleasure of receiving your letter of the 8th. instant by the last mail, in reply to which I have to inform you that the committee of ways & means, to whom the application on behalf of the University was referred, reported, sometime ago, a Bill remitting the *whole amount* of duties charged upon the late importation of manufactured marble for the use of the University. This Bill, in the prescribed course of proceeding here, was committed to a committee of the whole House, & now stands among the orders of the day for that committee. As however, in the arrangement of these orders, according to priority of time, many other Bills stood in advance of it, we have not yet been able to reach it, in the regular progress of our business. In the hope which I have continued to indulge from day to day, that we should soon reach it & dispose of it, I have heretofore delayed writing to you, that I might have it in my power, when I did so, to communicate something decisive. —— The indications of sentiment disclosed in the committee which reported the Bill, & the favorable dispositions manifested by the members of the House with whom I have conversed upon the subject, as well as the intrinsic merits of the application, encourage me to believe that there can be but little doubt of it's success. You may rely on my constant attention & diligent endeavors to procure as early a decision as possible. — It does not appear from the papers you sent me, when the Bond or Bonds given to secure the payment of the duties, become due. If the day of payment should be an early one, that consideration would justify a motion to take up the Bill before it's regular time.— I will give you the earliest information of our farther proceedings upon this subject . . . .

82. B. of V, T.J.'s hand; April 7, 1826

. . . . If the duties on the imported marble should be remitted by Congress, the Executive Committee are authorised to procure a clock and bell for the use of the University.

83. T.J., Monticello, to Arthur S. Brockenbrough; May 2, 1826; JP-2316

I was just getting on my horse to see you when some members of Congress arrive and keep me at home. I am obliged therefore to request you to come to me as it is of great necessity I should see you today if possible. We are called on by the Collector of Boston for immediate payment of our bond, due, as he says, the 6th instant. I must answer by tomorrow's mail.

84. T.J., Monticello, to Arthur S. Brockenbrough; May 5, 1826; JP-2317

When in conversation with you yesterday, I omitted to recommend what I had intended, that is, considering the difficulties of getting up the Capitels, to get the bases first hauled and set the bricklayers immediately to begin the columns. while about them you can get the Capitels in time.

The leaks in the roof we must remedy. as soon as Gen¹. Cocke comes I will consult with him what is to be done. my own opinion is in favor of another cover of tin laid on the old one without disturbing that. but Broke must be employed. we ought not to trust to people of whose skill we know nothing. the ignorance of the Frenchman is what costs us a new roof.

As soon as this is done we must cover the ill appearance of the plaistering by a whitewash, either of lime or Spanish white.

If you should be going to the mill I shall be glad if you would call on me. my ride yesterday has worsted me so much that I cannot repeat it, and I have recieved a letter which I cannot answer without a consultation with you. I shall send you soon a drawing of the Library tables for the Rotunda.

85. William C. Rives, Washington, to T.J.; May 13, 1826; JP-2320

I have now the satisfaction to inform you that the Bill, for remitting the duties demanded of the University, has passed the Senate, & has probably, by this time, received it's consummation as a law by the signature of the President.

The committee of the Senate, to which the Bill was referred, reported it with an amendment, the object of which was to provide for another case supposed by the committee to be precisely analogous; but as this case seemed to us to depend upon somewhat different principles from our's & there was reason to apprehend that it's incorporation might jeopardise the ultimate fate of the Bill, or, at least, produce farther delay in it's passage, we prevailed upon the committee to consent to the rejection of the amendment, & the Bill then passed, in it's original shape, without opposition. — As you informed me in your last letter, that the Bonds for the duties do not become due until after the middle of this month, I hope, notwithstanding the vexatious delays which have occurred in the progress of this business, it had been consummated in time to relieve you from any call for payment. — I send you a copy of the Bill, from which you will see the amount of duties directed to be refunded is $ 394.32. This is the full amount of duties paid on the 31 cases of marble for the use of the university (including as well the 19 cases of marble squares, as the 12 of marble bases), altho' I perceive in your letter adressed to us you put down the amount of duties paid, at $ 658.32. Your mistake arose from inadvertently consolidating the freight with the duties, as it shown in the following statement. —

The whole freight upon the 31 cases for the Un^{vy}, & the 6 cases for yourself was	$ 330.00
of which your portion for the six cases of mantels is	66.00
leaving for the freight upon the 31 cases for the Un^{vi}	$ 264.00
Add the amount of duties paid on the 31 cases	394.32
& it gives the amount stated in your letter	$ 658.32
Deduct the freight upon the 31 cases as above	264.00
& it gives the amount contained in the Bill	$ 394.32

.... As I expect to return to Albemarle in the course of a few days, I have thought it better to retain the papers you sent me, relating to the subject of the duties, in my personal custody, rather than commit them to the uncertainty & hazard of transmission by mail . . . .

86. T.J., Monticello, to John H. Cocke; May 20, 1826; JP-2321

Notes. the Dome leaks so that not a book can be trusted in it until remedied. this is from the ignorance of the workman employed. how shall it be remedied? my opinion is by a new tin cover put on the present, to be done by Broke of Staunton whose competence to it we know. this will cost us 8. or 900. Dollars. I know nothing else which experience will justify . . . .

. . . . 4. Congress have remitted the duties on our marbles. we are now to take measures as to the clock . . . .

6. but a stimulus must be applied, and very earnestly applied, or consultations and orders are nugatory. come then, dear Sir, to our aid, as soon as possible. our books are in a dangerous state. they cannot be opened until the presses are ready, nor they be got ready, till the Dome room is rendered dry.

87. T.J., Instructions to Arthur S. Brockenbrough; *ca.* May, 1826; JP-2324

Instructions to Mr Brockenbrough.
I. Engage Mr Broke to come immediately & put another cover of tin on the Dome-room of the Rotunda, without disturbing the old one.
2. the inside plaistering will then be to be coloured uniform with whiting.
3. the finishing the Dome room to be pushed by every possible exertion, as also the Anatomical building, by employing all the hands which can be got . . . .
7. I shall also write to Boston to engage a clock and bell. but I must be furnished immediately with very exact measures of the dimensions of the tympanum of the portico of the Rotunda, that is to say of it's base and perpendicular, to wit the lines a.b. & c.d. also the diameter & depth of the well, for the descent of the weights.

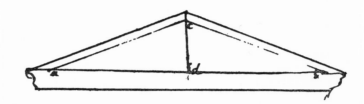

88. T.J., Monticello, to Joseph Coolidge, Jr.; June 4, 1826; JP-2325; pp

You have heretofore known that the ability of the University to meet the necessary expences of a bell and clock, depended on the remission by Congress, of the duties on the marble bases and capitels used in our buildings, a sum of nearly 3000.D. the remission is granted, and I am now authorized to close with Mr Willard for the undertaking of the clock, as proposed in your letter of Ag. 25. I must still however ask your friedly intermediacy, because it will so much abridge the labors of the written correspondence. for there will be many minutiae which your discretion can direct, in which we have full confidence, and shall confirm as if predirected. I have drawn up the material instructions, on separate papers which put into Mr Willard's hands, will, I trust leave little other trouble for you. we must avail ourselves of his offer (expressed in the same letter) to come himself and set it up, allowing the compensation which I am sure he will make reasonable. the dial-plate had better be made at Boston, as we can prepare our aperture for it, of sixty inches, with entire accuracy. we wish him to proceed with all practicable dispatch, and we are ready to make him whatever advance he usually requires; and we would rather make it immediately, as we have a sum of money in Boston which it would be more convenient to place in his hands at once, than to draw it here and have to remit it again to Boston. — if it would be out of his line to engage for the Bell also, be so good as to put it into any hands you please, and to say what we should advance for that also.

89. T.J., Monticello, to Arthur S. Brockenbrough; June 22, 1826; JP-2327

Mr Willard undertakes our clock, and without regard to price says that it shall be as good a one as the hands of man can make. he will come & set it up, observing that the accuracy of the movement of a clock depend as much on it's accurate and solid setting up as on it's works. he chuses to purchase the bell himself & says that one of 400. lb. is suff^t. for all our purposes. the whole amount will be 800 for the clock, 150. for the bell and his expences travelling and here, which may make the whole 1000.D. of which ¼ is to be remitted now immediately, having already incurred considerably on his own acc^t. by having wheels and other parts cast of chosen iron. 250. to be called for at his convenience, and the balance on the completion of the whole which will be in September. be so good therefore as to have the first remittance immediately made to Mr Joseph Coolidge J^r of Boston for Mr Willard whose C^n. name is unknown to me

90. B of V; Oct. 3-7, 1826

. . . . Resolved that the faculty be requested forthwith to cause the small room on the first floor of the rotunda to be finished & fitted for the reception of the natural and artificial curiosities given to the University by the late venerable Rector; and to have them suitably arranged for preservation & exhibition . . . .

Report to the Literary Fund
. . . . the Library Room in the Rotunda has been nearly completed, and the books put into it. Two rooms for the Professors of Natural Philosophy and Chemistry, and one large lecture room have also been fitted for use. The work of the Anatomical Hall is so far advanced that it may be used early in the next session. The Portico of the Rotunda has been finished, with the exception of

the flight of steps and the laying of the marble flags, which have been received and paid for. The work remaining to be done, is the finishing of one large oval room, one small one, and the entrance Hall of the Rotunda with the unfinished parts of the Portico and about one fourth of the Anatomical Hall. Some small additions are also necessary for the better accomodations of the Professors in their Pavilions, and of the students in their Dormitories, and for a few other minor objects.

91. B of V; July 18, 1827

. . . . Resolved That the Procetor shall cause a neat iron railing to be placed on the right and left of the portico of the Rotunda & adjacent to the same; so as to exclude access for the purpose of walking over the gymnasia . . . .

92. B of V; Oct. 3, 1828

. . . . Resolved that the objects of Mr Jefferson's donation be removed from the small oval room on the first floor of the Rotunda, to the small oval room in the basement story of the same building . . . .
Resolved That so much of the letter of the Proctor as related to the chimnies of the Rotunda, is referred to the Executive Committee, to be acted on as they may deem expedient.

93. Notes on drawings for Rotunda, T.J.'s hand; Plates VI, VIII, and IX

OBVERSE

[Plan for principal floor, in one of two larger rooms,]
area 110. sq. ft.

REVERSE

Rotunda reduced to the proportions of the Pantheon and accomodated to the purposes of a Library for the University with rooms for drawing, music, examinations and other accessory purposes.

The diameter of the building 77. feet, being ½ that of the Pantheon, consequently ¼ it's area, & ⅛ it's volume.
the Circumference 242.f.

		f			
the height.	foundation	3 - 0	foundation	3 - 0
	basement	7 - 6	basement	7 - 6
	Columns	28 - 6	lower rooms	17 -
	entablature	5 - 7¼	to spring of arch	18 - 4¼
	Attic	13 - 9	to top of wall	12 - 6
		58 - 4¼ = 58.35		58 - 4¼
		bricks		

3½ bricks thick	3	x 42 x 242 =	30,492
3	7½	x 36 x 242	65,340
2½	17	x 30 x 242	123,420
2	18- ... 4½	x 24 x 242	106,608
1½	12- ... 6	x 18 x 242	54,450

the whole circular external wall	380,310
2. massive chimnies, serving as buttresses	44,800
front & back buttresses of 141.f. area each	263,375
3 semielliptical partitions of 2. bricks thick	108,450
	796,835

shafts of 12. columns
f   f
3. diam. 23½ high   315,840

1,112,675

to thicken the walls a half brick more from bottom to top adds 84702 brick making the whole 1,197,377 or say 1,200,000 which is advisable

	Module	f		
diameter	1	= 3.		
dimin^d diam.	0 - 54	= 2 - 8.4		
base	30	= 1 - 6)	f	i
shaft	7 - 40	=23 - 6) =	28 - 6	
capitel	1 - 10	= 3 - 6)		

architrave	38	= 1 -10.8)	
frize	28½	= 1 - 5.1)	5 - 7.2
cornice	45½	= 2 - 3.3)	

	parts		
Attic base	121	3)	
shaft	363	9)	13 - 9
surbase	69	1 - 9)	
			48 - 0

                           f   i

diam. of Attic pilaster   2 - 8.4

intercolonnation 2. dia. = 6 f

                                  f   i

                         /

projection of Cornice 47 ¾ = 2 - 4.65

                   f   i

Pediment. span 52 - 5.5

       height 11 - 8

              mod   f

breadth of Portico 16 = 48

plinths of Dome 11. f

crown of d⁰ -   8. f

              19. f

Internal heights	f	
foundation	3 -	
pedestal or basement	7 - 6	
floor, or step	1 -	
lower rooms clear	16 -	
floor	1 -	
library. wall	29 - 6)	48 - 6 height of dome room
clear of dome above that	19 -)	
	77 -	

Library.

    to get a circle or columns at a proper distance from the wall and with their [illegible word] is the height of the wall within, to the spring of the arch the diameter must 1 - 6 the rad——? they are arranged must be 27. f (or 54. f diam.) circumference 113. diameters = 169.5 to correspond with the windows there must be 20. intercollonnations. and that the intercolonnations may not be too large for the Corinthian order we must use an intercolonnation of 3.

                                                             f

diameters will be   4 - 6

2 columns   3 -

                      /

space between them 40   1 -

                                             8 - 6

[The following is on the reverse of Illustration IX]

Additional Notes for the Library.
the estimate of bricks on the first drawing was   1,112,675
if we make the wall half a brick thicker from bottom
                                        to top it adds   84,702
                                                                 1,197,377.

If we make the Attic of wood, instead of bricks,
                                        it deducts   79,920

leaving the corrected estimate for the whole Rotunda   1,117,457.

the Terras on each side is to be in breadth equal to the flank
of the Portico.
it will be 61 - 6, but deducting for the descent of the steps it may be
consid^d as 54 f. long
the foundation & Basement being 2. brick thick & 10½ f. high &
4 such walls   54,432

so that the Building & it's 2. terrasses will take   1,171,889.

the thickness of the wall at top, to wit, at the spring of the Vault of the roof
is 22. i. on the top of the wall lay a curbed plate, in Delorme's manner, consist-
ing of 4. thicknesses of 3. i. each. 22. i. wide, pieces 12. f. long, breaking joints
every 3. f. bolted through with bolts of iron having a nut & screw at their end.
on this curved plate the ribs of the roof are to rest.
the ribs are to be 4. thicknesses of 1. i. plank, in pieces 4. f. long, breaking joints
at every foot. they are to be 18. i. wide, which leaves 4. i. of the plate for the
Attic uprights to rest on
the ribs are to be keyed together by cross boards at proper intervals from the
ribs to head in as they shorten the curb of the sky light to be made also in
Delorme's way, but vertically.
the fireplaces & chimnies must be brought forward so that the flues may not make
a hollow in the main walls.
they will thus become buttresses.

94. 3rd, 4th, and 39th pages, Operations at and for the College, T.J.'s hand;
JP-1518

The Concave cieling of the Rotunda is proposed to be painted skyblue
and spangled with gilt stars in their position and magnitude copied exactly
from any selected hemisphere of our latitude. a seat for the Operator movable
and fixable at any point in the concave will be necessary, and means of giving
every star it's exact position.

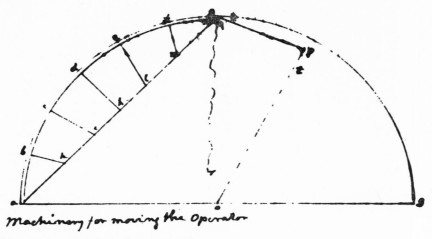

Machinery for moving the Operator

Machinery for moving the Operator

a.b.c.d.e.f.g. is the inner surface of 90° of the dome.

o.p. is a boom, a white oak sapling of proper strength, it's heel working in the center of the sphere, by a compound joint admitting motion in any direction like a ball and socket.

p.q.r. is a rope suspending the small end of the boom, passing over a pulley in the zenith at g. and hanging down to the floor by which it may be raised or lowered to any altitude.

at p. a common saddle with stirrups is fixed for the seat of the operator and seated on that he may by the rope be presented to any point of the concave. Machinery for locating the stars.

a.s. is the horizontal plane passing thro the center of the sphere o. an annular ream of wood, of the radius of the sphere must be laid on this plane and graduated to degrees and minutes, the graduation beginning in the North rhomb of the place. call this the circle of amplitude. a movable meridien of 90°. must then be provided, it's upper end moving on a pivot in the xenith, it's lower end resting on the circle of amplitude. this must be made of thin flexible white oak like the ream of a cotton spinning wheel, and fixed in it's curvature, in a true quadrant by a similar lath of white oak as it's chord a.n. their ends made fast together by clamps. this flexible meridian may be of 6. i. breadth and graduated to degrees and minutes.

the zenith distance and amplitude of every star must then be obtained from the astronomical tables. place the foot of the movable meridian in that of the North rhomb of the place, and the polar star at it's zenith distance, and so of every other star of that meridian. then move the foot to another meridian at a convenient interval, mark it's stars by their zenith distance and so go round the circle.

bh. ci. dk. el. fm. are braces of window cord for keeping the meridian in it's true curve.

perhaps the rope had better be attached to the boom at s. instead of p. to be out of the way of the operator perhaps also the chord *an* had better present it's edge to the meridian than it's side.

if the meridian ark and it's chord be 6.i. wide & ½ i. thick they will wiegh about 135. lb. and consequently be easily manageable.

if the boom op. be 35. f. long, 6. i at the but and 3. i. at the small end, it might weigh about 100. lb. and be manageable also.

Rotunda. notes.

the rule for apportioning the area of windows to the volume of the room is to take the cubic contents of the room in feet, and the square root of that for the area of all it's windows.

the large oval room below has 17,600 cub. f. contents

the sq. root of that is 132 sq. f for all it's windows. each of the 4. windows then must be $\frac{132}{4}$ = 33. f or say they must be 4. f. wide, & 8 f. high.

the body of the house (shaft & entablature) being 34 - 1½ high & the voids of the 2. windows (below & above) being 16. f. is in good proportion, being nearly one half.

95. Notes on drawing for Gymnasia, T.J.'s hand; Plate XIII

OBVERSE

drawing for arcade for gymnasia on either side of the Rotunda. [T.J.'s hand?]

REVERSE

	f	i
the opening of the arches in breadth	6	5½
the breadth of the piers	2	3½
	8	9

the piers joining the Portico are of double breadth.

whole length of Gymnasium 84. f

there are 9. arches on a side -

Heights of the N. facade of the Gymnasiua 12 - 2

from floor of Gymnasium to floor of Portico			12 - 2

	f	i	
height of pier	6	9	
Arch	2	9	
architrave		9 ¾	
Keystone		1 ¼	
rooflets	2		12 - 2

Basement on the South side

from floor of Gymnasium to level of lawn	4 - 2	
to bottom of arch	1 - 10	
Arch	3 - 3	
architrave & key stone	11	
rooflets	2	12 - 2

for the piers of the arches

		i	
base. zocle		13	
listel		6½	19½
dye			48¾
impost			9¾

Apr. 26. 24.

it was afterwards agreed 18. i. would suffice for the rooflets on the North side which would admit the arches on that side to be semicircles.

[NOTE: the following is not in T.J.'s hand, perhaps the Proctor's (?)]

	ft in
Width of the Arches	6 - 4.6
breadth of the piers	3 - 2.3
the outside piers are	5 - 3.55

ft

From the front of the pavilions to the pedestal of the Rotunda 83 the thickness of the wall —— makes the whole extend 84 ft

	ft in		ft in
8 arches of	6 - 4.6	=	51 0.8
7 piers breadth	3 - 2.3	=	22 - 4.1
2 on the flank	5 - 3.55	=	10 7.1

84 - 0

96. Notes on drawing for Clock & Bell, T.J.'s hand; Illustration XIV

OBVERSE

plan of a Clock for the Rotunda, the bell to serve for ringing also. the bell to be fixed immoveable on a forked stem on the ridge pole of the portico.
it's dial plate to be in the center of the tympanum of the Pediment
the bell tongue to vibrate in the vertical plane formed by itself and the bell rope
the Clock hammer to vibrate * within the bell in a plane between the last & that of the * ridge pole.
the clock weights to descend in the cylindrical cavities of the wall on each side. the bell rope is one of them.
the clock to have an hour hand only with divisions for 60'. between each hour.
if the plate be 7.f. diam. the hours will be 22.i. and the minutes 0.266 i
to be wound up on the back side of the works
side view showing bell hammer. b.
* the stem forks as well for stability as to make a vacancy for the bell tongue to vibrate thro.
front view showing bell-tongue a.

PLATES

which, being made of timber, is not technically a vault although it assumes a vault shape. On it's inside surface it is a portion of a true sphere. An oculus appears in the center of the dome. The interior colonnade of the library room has a full establature on both sides and two balcony levels, the upper one with balustrade.

PLATE XIII. Arcade for the Gymnasia, North Elevation
Because of the use of wash, so little used by Jefferson, there is a possibility that this drawing may not be entirely, if at all, by him, although it is endorsed in his hand on the reverse side.

PLATE XIV. Clock and Bell for Rotunda, T.J.'s hand.

PLATE XV. Book I, Plate XXIII, PALLADIO, 1721. ". . . . taking the base however from his plate 23 . . . ." (See Doc. 16).

PLATE XVI. Book I, Plate XXV, PALLADIO, 1721. ". . . . that [the base] of Pl. 25. having too much work as well as that of the Pantheon . . . ." (See Doc. 16).

PLATE XVII. Book I, Plate XXVI, PALLADIO, 1721. ". . . . my original drawing for the main entablature . . . . that of Palladio Book. 1. Pl. 26 . . . ." (See Doc. 16).

PLATE XVIII. Book I, Plate XXXV, PALLADIO, 1721. ". . . . his plates 35. 36. give the handsomest entablatures for windows . . . . adopt the architrave at the left hand bottom corner of pl. 35. give it a plain frize instead of his swelled one, and the dentil cornice at the bottom of pl. 36 . . . ." (See Doc. 16).

PLATE XIX. Book I, Plate XXXVI, PALLADIO, 1721. See Note for previous illustration.

PLATE XX. Book IV, Plate LX, PALLADIO, 1721. Corinthian Order of the Pantheon.
"all to be copied exactly from those of the Pantheon, as represented by Palladio. B. 4. 20. pl. 60. Leoni's edition" (See Doc. 26).

PLATE XXI. Book I, Plate XXX, PALLADIO, 1721. Composite Order.
"to be copied from Palladio B. 1. c. 18. pl. 30." (See Doc. 26).

PLATE XXII. Bond for Duties on the Marble.

INDEX

PLATES

PLATE I

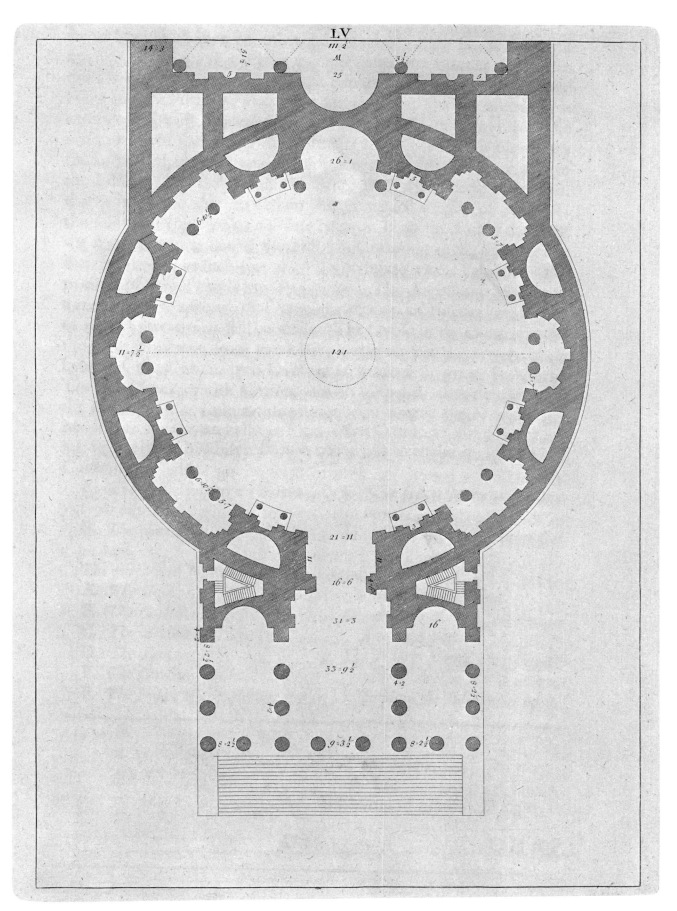

Plan of the Pantheon; Palladio

PLATE II

Elevation of the Pantheon; Palladio

PLATE III

LVIII.

Side Elevation of Portico of the Pantheon; Palladio

PLATE IV

LIX.

Lateral Section of Portico of the Pantheon; Palladio

PLATE V

LXI.

Metà del diametro ; Piedi 60 e Oncie 6.

B. Picart sculp. devenit 1719.

Section of the Pantheon ; Palladio

PLATE VI

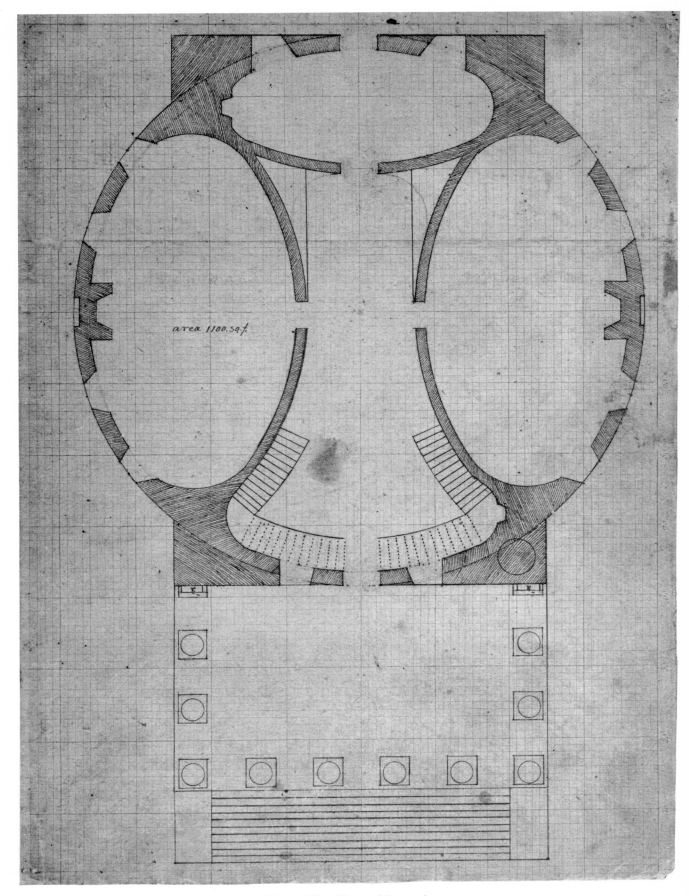

area 1100.sq.f.

Plan of First Floor of Rotunda

PLATE VII

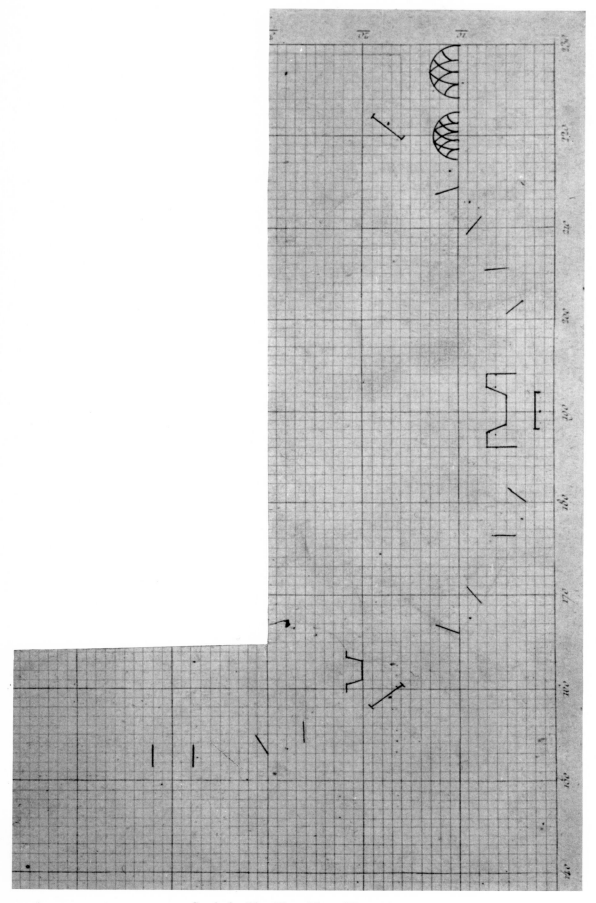

Study for First Floor Plan of Rotunda

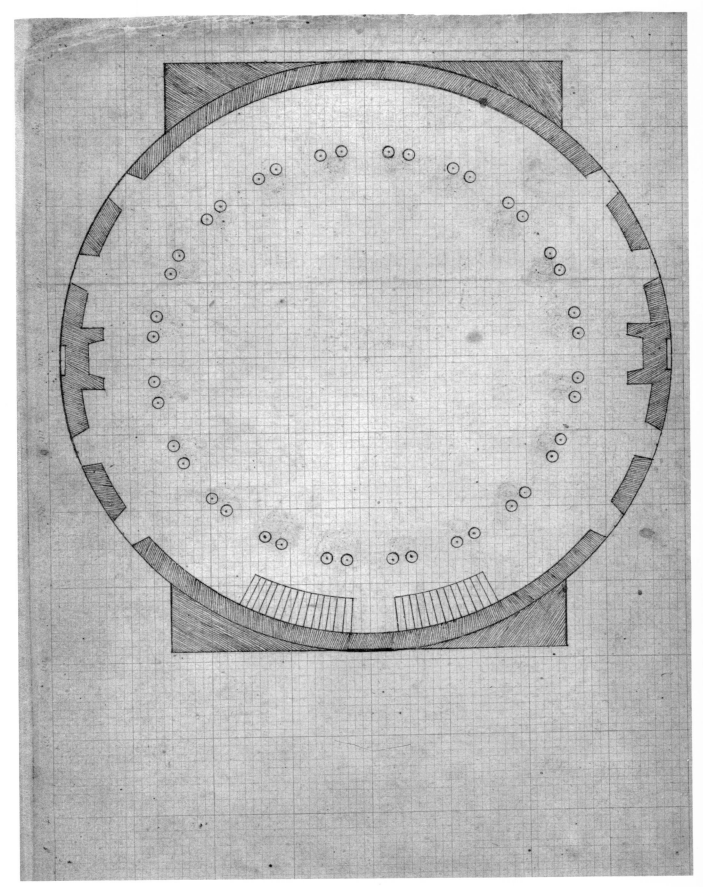

PLATE VIII

Plan of Second Floor of Rotunda

PLATE IX

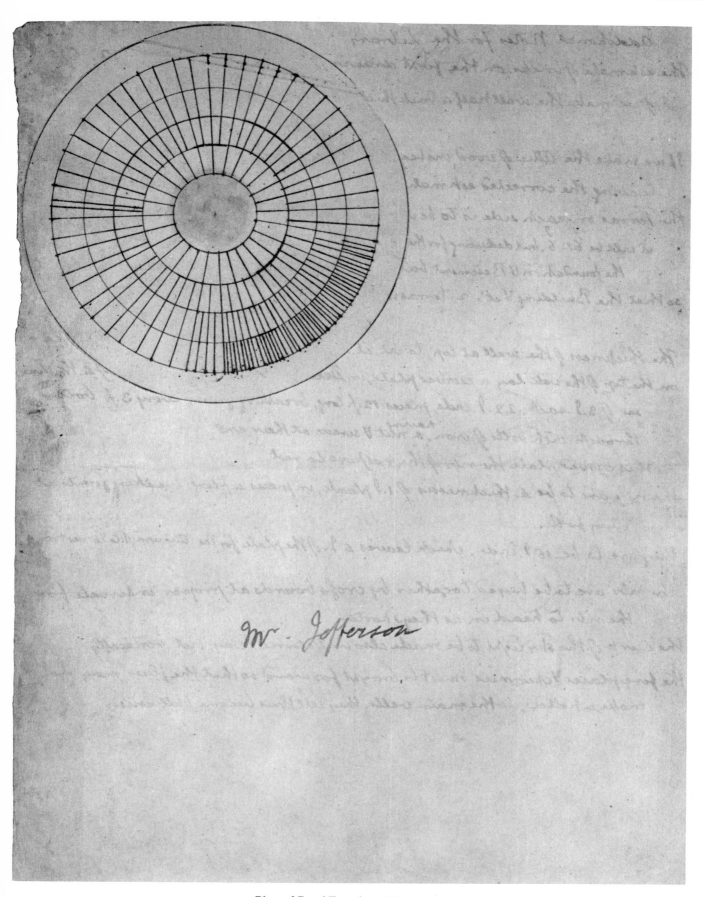

Plan of Roof Framing of Rotunda

PLATE X

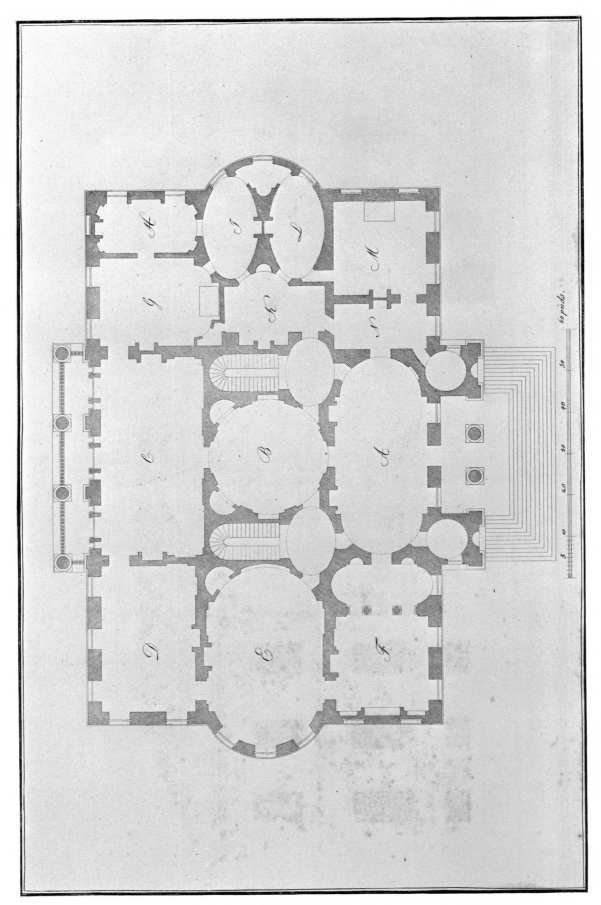

Plate 13 ; Stieglitz

PLATE XI

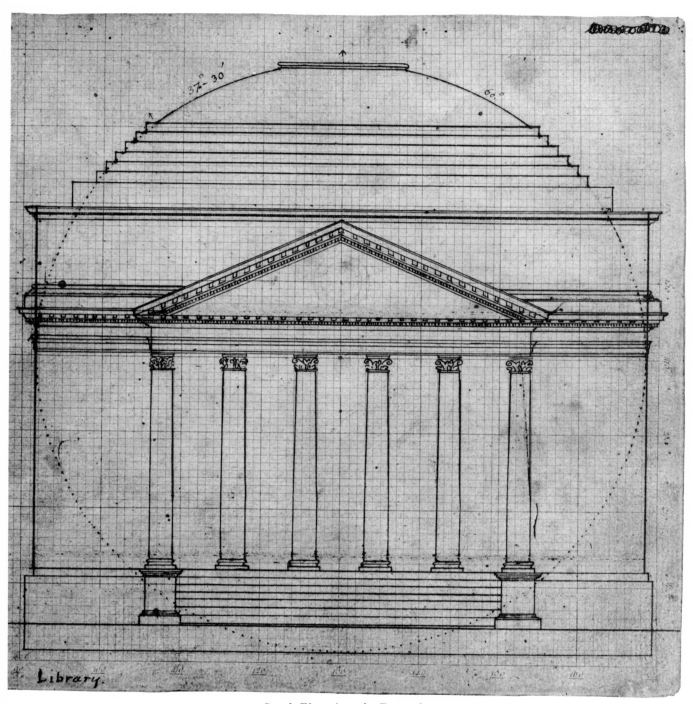

South Elevation, the Rotunda

PLATE XII

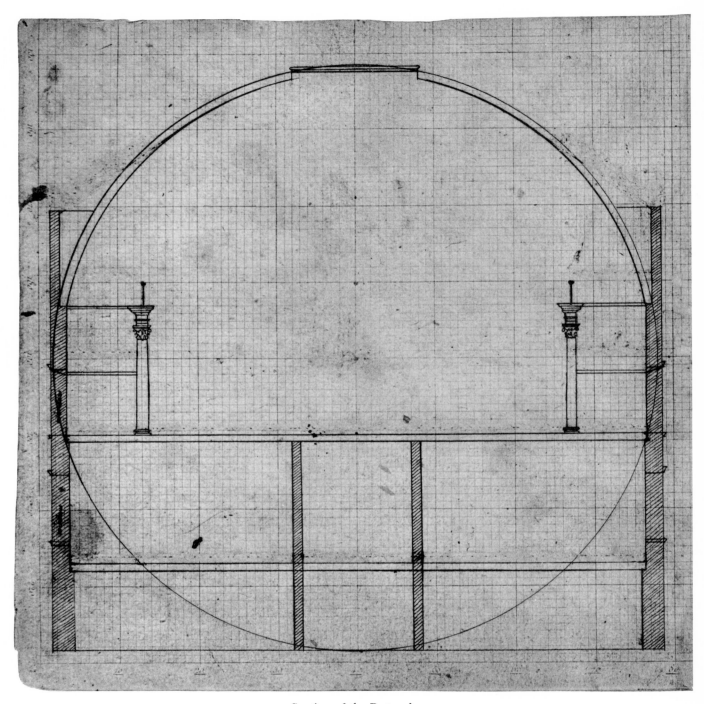

Section of the Rotunda

PLATE XIII

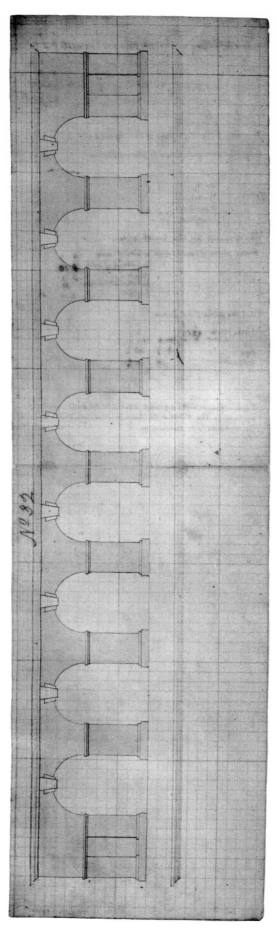

North Elevation of the Arcade for the Gymnasia

PLATE XIV

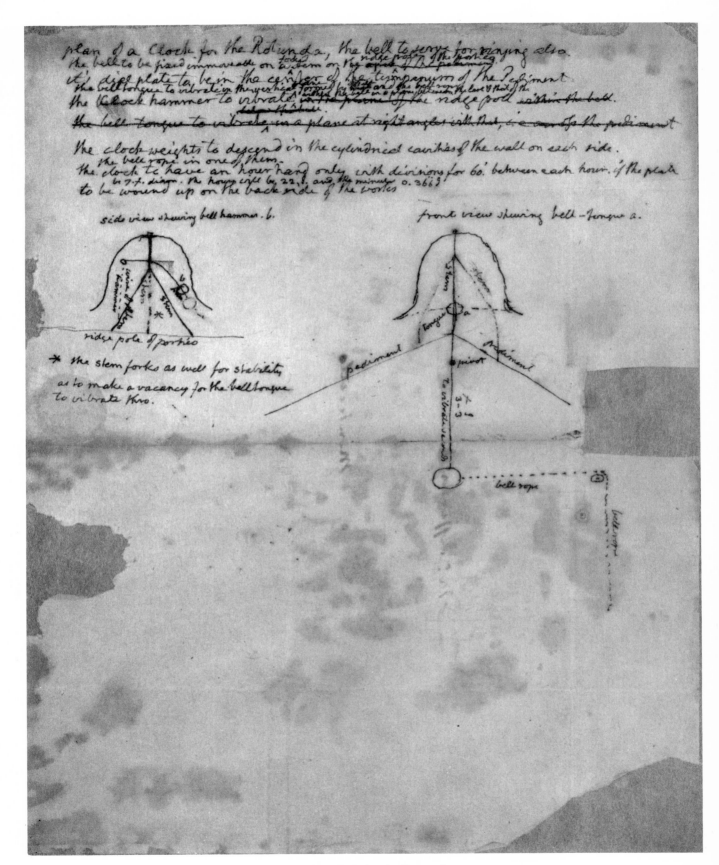

Clock and Bell for the Rotunda

PLATE XV

Book I, Plate XXIII; Palladio

PLATE XVI

Book I, Plate XXV; Palladio

PLATE XVII

Book I, Plate XXVI; Palladio

PLATE XVIII

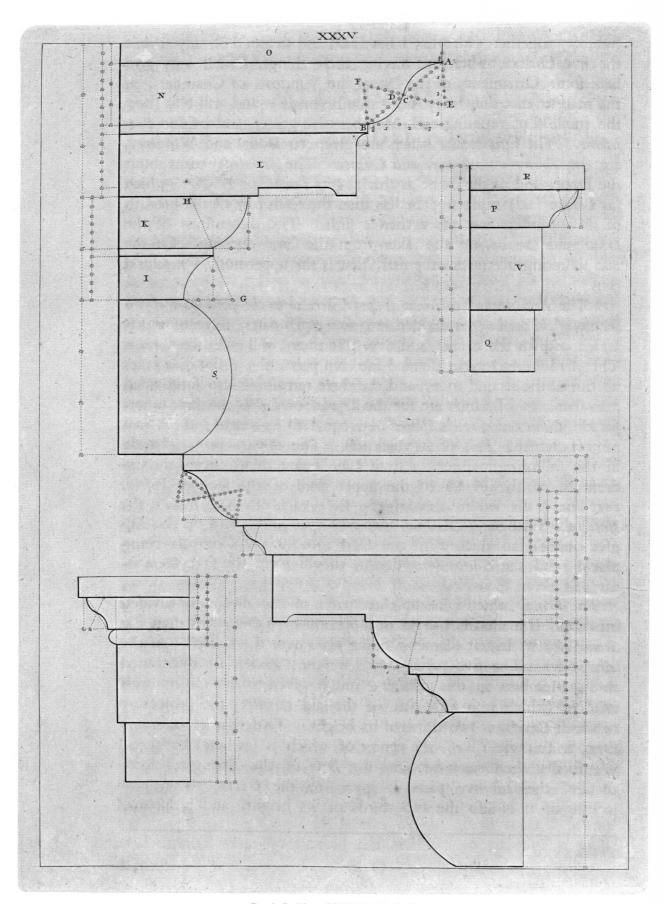

Book I, Plate XXXV; Palladio

PLATE XIX

XXXVI

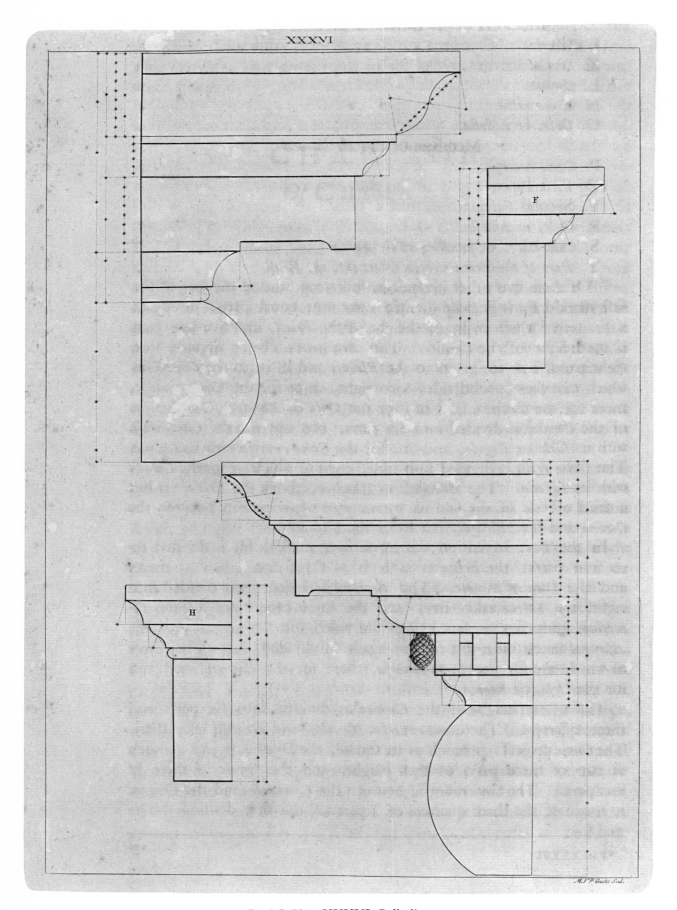

Book I, Plate XXXVI; Palladio

PLATE XX

Book IV, Plate LX; Palladio

PLATE XXI

Book I, Plate XXX; Palladio

PLATE XXII

MAN. 532

Know all Men by these Presents....that

We,

Thomas Jefferson, John H. Cocke James Madison Chapman Johnson, James Breckenridge, George Loyall and Joseph C. Cabell

are held and firmly bound to the UNITED STATES OF AMERICA, in the sum of FIFTY THOUSAND DOLLARS, to be paid to the United States ; for payment whereof, we bind ourselves, our heirs, executors and administrators, jointly and severally, firmly by these Presents,— Sealed with our seals. Dated this *12* ——————————— day of *October* —— in the fiftieth year of the Independence of the said United States, in the year of our Lord one thousand eight hundred and twenty-five.

THE Condition of this Obligation is such, That if the above bounden

Thomas, John H. James Madison, James Breckenridge Chapman, George and Joseph C.

or either of them, or either of their heirs, executors, or administrators, shall and do, on or before the *Sixth* —— day of *May* —— next, well and truly pay, or cause to be paid, unto the Collector of the Customs for the District of *Boston* and *Charlestown*, for the time being, the sum of *Two Thousand Fifty Seven* ——————————— Dollars, and *fifteen* ——————— Cents, or the amount of the duties to be ascertained as due, and arising on certain Goods, Wares and Merchandise entered by the above bounden *Thomas* as imported in the *Brig Farnworth* *J. Warner* Master, from *Genoa & Leghorn* as per entry dated this date then the above obligation to be void, otherwise to remain in full force and virtue.

Sealed and Delivered
in the presence of

Arthur S Brockenbrough *Th. Jefferson*
Proctor of the University of V. *John H. Cocke*
James Madison
C. Johnson
James Breckinridge
Geo Loyall
Joseph C. Cabell

GOOD FOR

Bond for Duties on the Marble

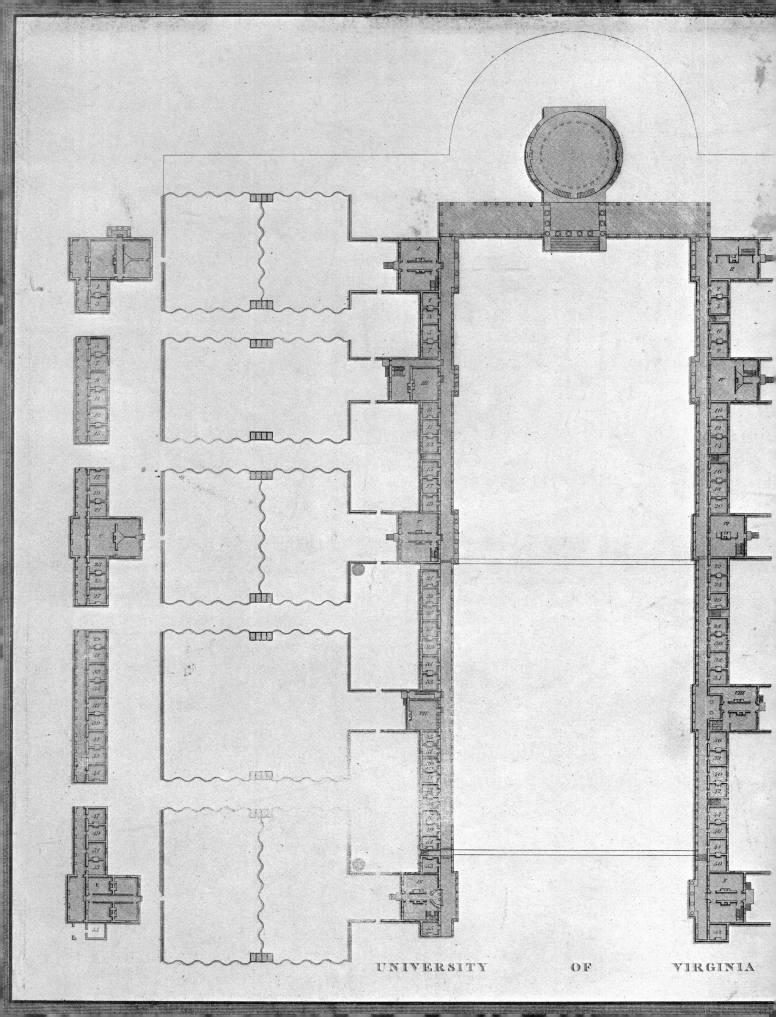

UNIVERSITY OF VIRGINIA